S. HRG. 113–527

PROTECTING OUR CHILDREN'S MENTAL HEALTH: PREVENTING AND ADDRESSING CHILDHOOD TRAUMA IN INDIAN COUNTRY

HEARING

BEFORE THE

COMMITTEE ON INDIAN AFFAIRS
UNITED STATES SENATE

ONE HUNDRED THIRTEENTH CONGRESS

SECOND SESSION

———

NOVEMBER 19, 2014

———

Printed for the use of the Committee on Indian Affairs

U.S. GOVERNMENT PUBLISHING OFFICE

92–529 PDF   WASHINGTON : 2015

For sale by the Superintendent of Documents, U.S. Government Publishing Office
Internet: bookstore.gpo.gov Phone: toll free (866) 512–1800; DC area (202) 512–1800
Fax: (202) 512–2104 Mail: Stop IDCC, Washington, DC 20402–0001

COMMITTEE ON INDIAN AFFAIRS

JON TESTER, Montana, *Chairman*
JOHN BARRASSO, Wyoming, *Vice Chairman*

TIM JOHNSON, South Dakota
MARIA CANTWELL, Washington
TOM UDALL, New Mexico
AL FRANKEN, Minnesota
MARK BEGICH, Alaska
BRIAN SCHATZ, Hawaii
HEIDI HEITKAMP, North Dakota

JOHN McCAIN, Arizona
LISA MURKOWSKI, Alaska
JOHN HOEVEN, North Dakota
MIKE CRAPO, Idaho
DEB FISCHER, Nebraska

MARY J. PAVEL, *Majority Staff Director and Chief Counsel*
RHONDA HARJO, *Minority Deputy Chief Counsel*

CONTENTS

PROTECTING OUR CHILDREN'S MENTAL HEALTH: PREVENTING AND ADDRESSING CHILDHOOD TRAUMA IN INDIAN COUNTRY

WEDNESDAY, NOVEMBER 19, 2014

U.S. SENATE,
COMMITTEE ON INDIAN AFFAIRS,
Washington, DC.

The Committee met, pursuant to notice, at 2:30 p.m. in room 628, Dirksen Senate Office Building, Hon. Jon Tester, Chairman of the Committee, presiding.

OPENING STATEMENT OF HON. JON TESTER, U.S. SENATOR FROM MONTANA

The CHAIRMAN. I will call this hearing of the Senate Indian Affairs Committee to order.

This will be my last hearing as Chairman, hopefully for the short term, but the bottom line is I just want to thank the staffs of both the Majority and Minority for the work they have done.

We would not get a lot done around here if it wasn't for our staffs. I just want to say I appreciate their commitment to Indian Country.

It has been great in my short tenure as Chairman of this Committee to be able to get around and see some of the challenges out there. As was pointed out to me when I was first elected to the United States Senate, the challenges in Indian Country are many. There are so many that it really does take a bipartisan effort to get those solved.

I think this Committee has worked traditionally in a fairly good bipartisan way. We have some opportunities during this lame duck to get some stuff done for Indian Country and hopefully that will happen. Whether it is in the area of health, water, housing, police protection or whatever, these are very important issues.

To get down to the business at hand, I have been able to spend some time in Indian Country speaking with tribal leaders, hearing from concerned tribal members, and visiting celebrations and ceremonies that keep Indian Country alive and vibrant.

I must say I have enjoyed the time I spent in those communities. The diversity of Indian Country and the value that Indian Country places on its children to protect them and helping them to become future leaders for their people.

(1)

It is often said that children are our most precious resource. Nowhere is this more visible than in tribal communities I have visited.

Yet, some disturbing realities persist. Studies show that Native children suffer from high rates of trauma, abuse and exposure to violence. They grow up in poverty at levels much higher than our non-Native counterparts. These children are exposed to a cycle of trauma that I think we need to address together to break.

Earlier this week, the Department of Justice released a report entitled Ending Violence So Children Can Thrive, which outlined recommendations for addressing children exposed to violence. This report represents tireless research and work in the field of preventing childhood trauma and promoting resiliency in early childhood.

Both are crucial to building strong communities. Both will be vital in the future of our Native children. It is precisely reports like this with recommendations from tribal people that we need to see.

However, as we know all too well, it is more than words on paper that our children need. We need to turn these recommendations into actions, put safeguards in place for our most vulnerable community members.

There are tremendous studies on brain research, some of which we will hear about today, that show us how a child's brain development, social and emotional development are compromised when there are repeated and significant instances of fear, neglect and anxiety.

A 2008 report by the Indian Country Child Trauma Center calculated that Native youth are two-and-a-half times more likely to experience trauma when compared to their non-Native peers. This is preventable.

We have the power to ensure our children grow up in safe and supportive environments. We have the power to help support healthy and appropriate development and make it possible for our children to thrive. My hope is that is our focus today.

We have heard what is wrong. Now we need to hear what we need to do to make it right, what we need to do to make it right by our children. That should be the most important question we ask and that is the question I know hard working folks in Indian Country are asking themselves every day.

I look forward to this hearing from the Administration, education and tribal leaders who are here today about how issues of childhood trauma impact their respective agencies and communities and what we, as policymakers, can do better to help protect and promote resiliency among our Native children.

As many of you have noticed, we originally scheduled two panels but we have one now because we have a vote a number of votes at 3 o'clock. We shortened the time frame to be able to give us a few more minutes for questions.

With that, I would be remiss if I did not recognize the Vice Chairman, with whom it has been a pleasure to serve with over the past almost a year. With that, you can give your opening statement, Senator Barrasso.

STATEMENT OF HON. JOHN BARRASSO,
U.S. SENATOR FROM WYOMING

Senator BARRASSO. Thank you, Mr. Chairman.

I just want to say how much I appreciate your leadership. You have been committed to Indian issues your entire career in the Senate, even more so as Chairman. The Montana tribes have benefitted greatly from your work.

I want to thank you for your work and ask you all to join me in thanking the Chairman as this is his final hearing.

I also want to tell you that I appreciate you holding this hearing. I agree with your very thoughtful comments.

According to the Indian Health Service, childhood trauma is disproportionately experienced by Indian children. The reasons are multi-factorial, related to recurrent abuse, accompanied with high incidences of alcohol and drug abuse, suicide, violence and according to substance abuse and mental health services of the Administration, the death of family members can also be a significant cause of childhood trauma.

These factors are particularly acute on the Wind River Reservation in Wyoming. The Indian Health Service has informed this Committee that the average age of death on the Wind River Reservation in Wyoming is 49 years of age.

Alcohol-related injuries have been cited by the Indian Health Service as a significant contributing factor for the premature death rate. This is a sensitive matter and one that will require active participation from multiple disciplines and agencies to address.

The Attorney General has established an advisory committee to his Task Force on American Indian and Alaska Native Children Exposed to Violence. The advisory committee was charged with examining this exposure to violence and providing recommendations on how to address the issue.

Yesterday, the advisory committee issued its policy recommendations to the Department of Justice so I look forward to examining how those recommendations will address and prevent trauma to Indian children.

I want to thank the witnesses and look forward to your testimony.

Thank you, Mr. Chairman.

The CHAIRMAN. Thank you, Senator Barrasso.

Are there other opening statements? Senator Cantwell.

STATEMENT OF HON. MARIA CANTWELL,
U.S. SENATOR FROM WASHINGTON

Senator CANTWELL. Thank you, Mr. Chairman.

I too want to applaud your leadership. As Chairman of this Committee, you have certainly worked to improve economic opportunities, schools and obtain greater access to health care for tribal communities.

We certainly will look forward to working with you in the new Congress in your capacity to continue to work on these issues.

I certainly come to this hearing with still a heavy heart but am very thankful that you are having this hearing. As many know, Washington State suffered a devastating tragedy last month at the

Marysville Pilchuck High School that took the lives of five students, including the shooter.

Three of those shooting victims were members of the Tulalip Tribe of Washington. Across Washington and across tribal communities, we continue to mourn this incredible tragedy.

We will never know what exactly led to this senseless violence but it is a deadly and urgent reminder that we must do more to ensure the mental health system can help diagnose and treat young people when they need help.

The Marysville shooting is tragic proof of an alarming statistic. According to the Department of Justice, assaults, homicide and suicide account for 75 percent of the deaths of American Indians and Alaska Natives between the age of 12 and 20. This is unacceptable.

A robust mental health infrastructure is one key piece necessary to prevent these tragedies in the future. To that end, I would like to hear from the panelists how we can better integrate mental health and primary care services to make sure young people are not just turned away when they seek care.

The State of Washington is revamping its Medicaid delivery system to merge behavioral health and primary health care services by 2020. I would like to know what the Indian Health Service is working on to also integrate those kinds of behavioral health and primary care.

Unfortunately, data on the issues of psychiatric services available in Indian Country and data on the shortage are not widely available but a recent survey from Indian Health Services found there were only 950 psychiatric beds to serve all tribal communities across the United States of America.

We have to do better, Mr. Chairman. Thank you so much for this important hearing.

The CHAIRMAN. Are there other opening statements? Senator Begich?

STATEMENT OF HON. MARK BEGICH,
U.S. SENATOR FROM ALASKA

Senator BEGICH. Mr. Chairman, I want to thank you for having this important hearing.

To Verné, thank you for being here all the way from Alaska. We appreciate it. Hopefully we will hear some positive and encouraging testimony on what we can do better.

Mr. Chairman, this is going to be my last meeting also in a different way. I just want to say thank you and also to Senator Akaka who was here originally when I came and Senator Cantwell who chaired this Committee.

We did a lot of work on Alaska issues, the Nation's First People issues and spent a lot of time in this Committee talking about the importance of a variety of issues that are important, not only to Alaska, but really across the country. It has been an honor to be here.

As mentioned, the Attorney General's Advisory Committee on American Indian and Alaska Native Children Exposed to Violence, that important report has now been released. It has incredible information for us, including the work by Val Davidson, Bethel and many others who have spent the time to help us understand what more we can do.

Mr. Chairman, I want to thank you for helping to move forward one piece of legislation, our Safe Families and Villages Act, something I worked on for the last six years. We were trying to get unanimous consent. I understand on the Democratic side there is not a problem but on the Republican side, there is.

We have redrafted and hopefully the Republicans will look at this. We have streamlined it and hope to again hotline a different version tonight that streamlines it and resolves the concerns that the Republicans have on this issue.

It is an important piece. When we passed VAWA, Alaska Native people were left out. All we want to do is fix it for Alaska Native people. That is all.

Half the tribes of the Nation are from Alaska, not by population but by tribes. It just seems fair that we want to fix it for all first people of this country, not just the lower 48.

Even though I would prefer a more robust Safe Families and Villages Act, we have streamlined it and cleaned it up to meet, I believe, the minority's objections. Hopefully they will see it tonight and agree to hotline it as it is an important piece for Alaska.

Let me also say, Mr. Chairman, the work that is still ahead of this Committee I will not be a part of obviously, but it is enormous. The first people of this country, from Alaska Natives to the first people of the lower 48 and Hawaiian Natives are important. Many times they are forgotten in the issues with which we deal with.

Sometimes we pass great legislation and then forget there are also the first people who are touched by what we do. I would encourage this body as they move forward that not only is it important to discuss these issues here in this Committee, but as we talk on the floor of the Senate and other committees we sit on, that we discuss the importance of the first people of this country.

Again, I am hopeful that the one remaining piece I think would create equity for Alaska Native people will hopefully be resolved tonight. We will see.

I want to thank the Chairman and lastly, all the staff. The staff does incredible work for us. Sometimes we get to say all kinds of stuff in this forum but at the end of the day, it is the people who sit on the walls behind us that do an enormous amount of work and make sure the issues we care about are brought to the forefront and also help us make sure we get bipartisan support to get things done.

Mr. Chairman, I want to thank you for the opportunity and past chairmen who have been here and given me the chance to talk about Alaska issues.

Thank you.

The CHAIRMAN. Senator Begich, I would just say you and I serve on a lot of the same committees in the United States Senate. I just want to thank you for all your work and dedication, especially to Indian Country. Bringing the Alaska perspective has been critically important as we look to serve all our Native American challenges.

Are there other opening statements? Senator Murkowski.

STATEMENT OF HON. LISA MURKOWSKI,
U.S. SENATOR FROM ALASKA

Senator MURKOWSKI. Thank you, Mr. Chairman.

I apologize that I was not able to hear not only the other statements from colleagues but particularly that of my colleague from Alaska.

I want to take this opportunity to thank him for his leadership on these issues that we both agree are critically important to the Native people of our State and not just the Native people of our State because I think we recognize that our Alaska Native communities really represent what is the heart of Alaska.

We see that come together at the annual convention and at the Alaska Federation of Natives. We see it when we are out in the villages, villages that I think face some of the most difficult living conditions anywhere in this country.

When you look at the cost, when you think of the environment and the social factors that are against them, yet there is resilience, a strength and a beauty in these people that is to be celebrated.

I appreciate the efforts that he has made on so many of these issues, working together and talking about the Safe Families and Villages Act, something that we have been working on for a period of years and our staffs have shared initiative on that.

He mentioned that there has been resistance on the Republican side of the aisle. That is correct. There are those who have waited to hear the comments coming back from the Department of Justice on this. We are still waiting on that. It has made it complicated.

I have committed to him, as I have committed to Alaskans, that one of the things we can do most certainly at this point in time is to repeal Section 910 of VAWA, absolutely Alaska-specific there, but I think an effort that goes a long way in ensuring that there is a level of equity for some of the most vulnerable.

We will certainly work on that and I am happy to take a look at the streamlined version that he just mentioned.

I also want to acknowledge the work of Senator Heitkamp. The hearing we are having today focusing on the mental health needs of our children within Indian Country, the leadership that has been demonstrated focusing on our Native children in the lower 48 as well as Alaska Natives, I think has stepped up the review to a point I have not seen in the 12 years I have been serving on this Committee.

I think it is because of the doggedness of the Senator from North Dakota in focusing on this. I am pleased that we have been able to move forward the Children's Commission.

We see too clearly in the statistics the impact of child abuse, of neglect, of trauma and see that not only with the children but as these children grow to be contributing members of society, to become parents and knowing that trauma is not limited to that instance and how that ripples across our families and across our communities.

We have some very, very troubling statistics in Alaska. Our Alaska Native Tribal Health Consortium Epidemiology Center has estimated that 75 percent of Alaska Native people have experienced adverse childhood experiences.

Senator Begich was with us in Fairbanks last year at the AFN convention when a group of young people from the village of Tanana took to the center stage of a convention of 4,000–5,000 people and basically said, we have had enough. We are tired of adults who are abusive, we are tired of the drinking, we are tired of the drugs, we are tired of adults who are not role models, and we are tired of the violence.

When it takes our young people to shame the grownups into action, we darned well better be paying attention. I thank those who have joined us, those who have traveled far. Ms. Boerner, thank you.

I also recognize we are going to have a whole series of votes. I don't know how we are going to get through this critically important hearing and get all the information out on the table but I thank you for having it, Mr. Chairman.

The CHAIRMAN. Thank you.

Senator Heitkamp.

STATEMENT OF HON. HEIDI HEITKAMP,
U.S. SENATOR FROM NORTH DAKOTA

Senator HEITKAMP. Very quickly, none of us can escape the statistics. They are out there every day. Now we have the most recent report but very few of us have lived those statistics.

I have met people who have. The President has met people who have. People on this Committee have met the living and breathing examples of those statistics.

If we, the powerful government of the United States, cannot protect the poorest, most disenfranchised and most vulnerable of all people, then we are not worthy of the seats we are sitting in. We are not worthy of where we are right now.

This will be our unending commitment. I want to thank my good friend, Senator Murkowski from Alaska, for sharing this burden with me. I came here knowing this was going to be among my highest priorities because I have seen the faces of those statistics and they will haunt me. They haunt anyone who really opens their eyes.

What you do is so important. I know the trauma you experience as first responders. I know that trauma because I have seen it. Thank you because you share that burden every day and you share the love for children. Hopefully you will share with us the solutions today.

Thank you so much.

The CHAIRMAN. Senator Franken.

STATEMENT OF HON. AL FRANKEN,
U.S. SENATOR FROM MINNESOTA

Senator FRANKEN. I want to associate myself with all the statements I have heard so far and thank Senator Begich.

I want to hear your testimony. I am sorry because of the votes, I would like to have this hearing again because I know we are not going to be able to do questions and answers. I will submit questions for the record but I want to get to your testimony.

I just want to associate myself with the three Senators I just heard and especially thank Senator Begich for his service and his friendship.

The CHAIRMAN. Thank you, Senator Franken and thank you all for your statements.

I don't know how this is going to work. We are going to listen to your opening statements and if we are pulled away, we may try to roll it for a while. Sometimes that works, sometimes it does not. We will see how it goes and see if we can get some Q and A in. Otherwise, the questions will be put forth in the record. The question will be in writing for you to answer at a later point in time and we will get them as part of the record.

I want to welcome our panelists. First, we have Robert L. Listenbee Jr., Administrator, Office of Juvenile Justice and Delinquency Prevention, U.S. Department of Justice. I also want to welcome back a friend of the Committee, Dr. Yvette Roubideaux, Acting Director, Indian Health Service.

We have Kana Enomoto, Principal Deputy Administrator, Substance Abuse and Mental Health Services Administration; Rick van den Pol, Director and Principal Investigator, Institute of Educational Research and Service, The University of Montana. This institute houses the National Native Children's Trauma Center and I want to thank you for traveling a distance to be here, Rick. Finally, we welcome Ms. Verné Boerner, President and CEO, Alaska Native Health Board in Anchorage, Alaska. Talking about a trip to come see us, thank you very much, Verné.

I would remind the witnesses to try to keep your testimony to five minutes and know that your full written testimony will be a part of the record.

We will start with you, Robert.

STATEMENT OF HON. ROBERT L. LISTENBEE JR., ADMINISTRATOR, OFFICE OF JUVENILE JUSTICE AND DELINQUENCY PREVENTION, U.S. DEPARTMENT OF JUSTICE

Mr. LISTENBEE. Thank you, Mr. Chairman.

Chairman Tester, Vice Chairman Barrasso, and other distinguished members of the Committee, I want to thank you for the opportunity to discuss childhood trauma in Indian Country.

The Department is committed to working with American Indian and Alaska Native communities and our partners to implement evidence-based approaches to preventing and addressing childhood trauma.

As the Administrator of the Office of Juvenile Justice and Delinquency Prevention at the Department of Justice, Office of Justice Programs, I oversee programs that provide direct assistance and services to American Indian and Alaska Native youth.

We work closely with tribal leaders, tribal elders and organizations to develop programs that take into account Native culture and practice.

Prior to my appointment as the OJJDP Administrator, I served as a public defender and trial lawyer for nearly 30 years and dedicated myself to seeking justice for youth involved in the juvenile justice system.

I represented hundreds of children and learned that many of the youth entering the juvenile justice system were likely exposed to some form of violence as children. More than 60 percent of kids in America encounter some form of violence, crime or abuse ranging from brief encounters as witnesses to serious violent episodes as victims.

As co-chair of the Attorney General's Task Force on Children Exposed to Violence, in 2012, the task force issued a final report containing comprehensive policy recommendations aimed at reducing children's exposure to violence and enhancing resiliency among affected children.

One of the primary recommendations was the establishment of a separate task force to address the significant problem of children's exposure to violence in American Indian and Alaska Native communities, recognizing the unique government-to-government relationship between the United States and tribes.

The Attorney General's Task Force on American Indian and Alaska Native Children Exposed to Violence, created in 2013, consisted of two components, the advisory committee and Federal working group. The department just received the recommendations from the advisory committee this week.

The advisory committee, co-chaired by Senator Byron Dorgan and Ms. Joanne Shenandoah, held four hearings including one held in Anchorage, Alaska, and six listening sessions nationwide.

They learned that American Indian and Alaska Native children experience various types of trauma at higher rates than other children, trauma that ranges from physical abuse as witnesses and victims to sex trafficking.

Alaska Natives are disproportionately affected by violent crime and their children are therefore disproportionately exposed to that violence. This difference can be attributed to vast regional distances across the State, geographical isolation, extreme weather, exorbitant transportation costs and lack of economic opportunity and access to resources.

Compounding these high rates of violence is historical trauma, a cumulative emotional and psychological wounding over the life span and across generations.

The advisory committee discovered that some tribes and urban Indian organizations have found ways to incorporate tradition and develop resources to protect their children from harm and help them heal. The integration of traditional healing practices into mental health prevention and treatment for Native children is essential.

In 2010, the Department of Justice launched its Coordinated Tribal Assistance Solicitation in direct response to tribes seeking a more streamlined, comprehensive grant process. CTAS gives tribes the flexibility needed to better address their criminal justice and public safety needs and funds initiatives such as the tribal youth programs.

In fiscal year 2014, the department awarded CTAS grants to 169 American Indian tribes, Alaska Native villages, tribal consortia and tribal designees. As part of the Attorney General's Defending Childhood Initiative, OJJDP funded initiatives in the Rosebud Sioux Tribe in South Dakota and the Chippewa Cree Tribe at the

Rocky Boy Reservation in Montana. I describe these projects in my written testimony.

OJJDP is also funding efforts to enhance the capacity of tribal healing to wellness courts to respond to alcohol-related issues of tribal youth.

The National Institute of Justice in partnership with OJJDP and OJP's Office of Victims of Crime is funding an effort to more effectively assess exposure to violence and victimization in American Indian and Alaska Native communities.

Mr. Chairman, I appreciate the opportunity to appear before you today and I am prepared to respond to any questions you may have.

[The prepared statement of Mr. Listenbee follows:]

PREPARED STATEMENT OF HON. ROBERT L. LISTENBEE JR., ADMINISTRATOR, OFFICE OF JUVENILE JUSTICE AND DELINQUENCY PREVENTION, U.S. DEPARTMENT OF JUSTICE

Introduction

Chairman Tester, Ranking Member Barrasso and other distinguished members of the Committee, thank you for this opportunity to discuss childhood trauma in Indian Country. As Administrator of the Office of Juvenile Justice and Delinquency Prevention (OJJDP) at the Department of Justice's Office of Justice Programs (OJP), I oversee programs that provide direct assistance and services to American Indian and Alaska Native youth. We work closely with tribal elders, tribal leaders and organizations to develop programs that take into account Native culture and practice.

Prior to my appointment as the OJJDP Administrator, I served as a public defender and trial lawyer for nearly 30 years and dedicated myself to seeking justice for youth involved in the juvenile justice system. I represented hundreds of children and made an important but unsettling observation: many of the youth entering the juvenile justice system were likely exposed to some form of violence as children. While more than 60 percent of kids in America encounter some form of violence, crime, or abuse, ranging from brief encounters as witnesses to serious violent episodes as victims,[1] limited research and anecdotal evidence suggest rates of crime and violence, in some tribal areas are higher.[2]

While serving as a Chief of the Juvenile Unit of the Defender Association of Philadelphia, I co-chaired the Attorney General's Task Force on Children Exposed to Violence.[3] In 2012, the Task Force issued a final report containing comprehensive policy recommendations[4] aimed at reducing children's exposure to violence and enhancing resiliency among affected children.[5] One of the primary recommendations was the establishment of a separate Task Force to address the significant problem of children's exposure to violence in American Indian and Alaska Native communities in a way that recognizes the unique government-to-government relationship between the United States and tribes.

---

[1] OJJDP Children's Exposure to Violence: A Comprehensive National Survey Bulletin, October 2009. *https://www.ncjrs.gov/pdffiles1/ojjdp/227744.pdf.*

[2] Perry, S.W., *American Indians and Crime (pdf, 56 pages),* A BJS Statistical Profile 1992–2002, Washington, D.C. : U.S. Department of Justice, Office of Justice Programs, Bureau of Justice Statistics, December 2004, NCJ 203097.

[3] In 2011, the Attorney General announced this Task Force as part of the Attorney General's Defending Childhood Initiative, a project that addresses the epidemic levels of exposure to violence faced by our nation's children. *http://www.justice.gov/defendingchildhood/task-force-children-exposed-violence.*

[4] Shortly after the release of the Task Force report, the Attorney general requested an Action Plan to implement the Task Force recommendations. The Action was developed and approved in 2013. The recommendations have been (and continue to be) acted upon by the Department and our federal partners.

[5] Listenbee, Robert L., Jr. et al., *Report of the Attorney General's National Task Force on Children Exposed to Violence,* Washington D.C.: U.S. Department of Justice, Office of Juvenile Justice and Delinquency Prevention, December 2012.

Attorney General's Task Force

In 2013, the Attorney General created the Task Force on American Indian and Alaska Native Children Exposed to Violence.[6] The Task Force consisted of two components:

- An Advisory Committee composed of non-federal subject matter experts who: (1) gathered information from public hearings, written testimony, site visits, listening sessions, and current research; and (2) used this information to draft a report to the Attorney General that includes recommendations to effectively address children's exposure to violence in Indian Country.[7]

- A Federal Working Group composed of federal officials from key agencies including the Departments of Justice, Interior, and Health and Human Services—who have experience with issues affecting American Indian and Alaska Native communities. This working group is in an ideal position to take steps to implement policy and programmatic changes for the benefit of American Indian and Alaska Native children exposed to violence.

While the Department just received the recommendations from the Advisory Committee this week, OJJDP has long been committed to partnering with tribal governments to improve public safety in communities and to building a better future for all young people.

The Advisory Committee, Co-Chaired by Senator Byron L. Dorgan and Ms. Joanne Shenandoah, held hearings in four locations (Bismarck, ND; Phoenix, AZ; Fort Lauderdale, FL; and Anchorage, AK) and six listening sessions nationwide which brought together national, regional, and local experts, solicited personal testimony, and provided a forum for discussion on the effects of exposure to violence and promising prevention and intervention strategies and programs.[8] During the hearings and listening sessions, the Advisory Committee learned that American Indian and Alaskan Native children experience various types of trauma at higher rates than other children—trauma that includes physical abuse (as witness and victims), sexual abuse, domestic violence, suicide, and victimization, and sex trafficking.

The Advisory Committee heard that Alaska Natives are disproportionately affected by violent crime and Alaska Native children are, therefore, disproportionately exposed to that violence. This difference can be attributed to vast regional distances across the state, geographical isolation, extreme weather, exorbitant transportation cost, and lack of economic opportunity and access to resources.

As one tribal leader told the Advisory Committee, "For us . . . the question is not who has been exposed to violence, it's who hasn't been exposed to violence."[9] Violence, including assaults, homicide, and suicide, accounts for 75 percent of deaths of American Indian and Alaska Native youth ages 12 to 20.[10] These serious adversities often lead to chronic and severe trauma. A recent report noted that tribal children and youth experience posttraumatic stress disorder (PTSD) at a rate of 22 percent.[11]

Compounding these high rates of violence in American Indian and Alaska Native communities is historical trauma: a cumulative emotional and psychological wounding over the life span and across generations. The Advisory Committee found that the degree of violence in American Indian and Alaska Native communities is directly related to historical trauma and the impact of policies and practices that have

---

[6] Task Force on American Indian and Alaska Native Children Exposed to Violence website: *http://www.justice.gov/defendingchildhood/task-force-american-indian-and-alaska-native-children-exposed-violence*

[7] It is noteworthy that while given their charge by the Attorney General, the Advisory Committee felt strongly that the problems facing children in American Indian and Alaska Native communities are so significant that only concerted action by the Executive branch agencies and Congress would begin to address them. Accordingly, they chose to address their recommendations to entities beyond the Department of Justice.

[8] American Indian and Alaska Native Children Exposed to Violence Hearing Testimony: *http://www.justice.gov/defendingchildhood/task-force-hearings*

[9] Mato Standing High, Attorney General of the Rosebud Sioux Tribe, quoted in Report of the Attorney General's National Task Force on Children Exposed to Violence, Dec. 12, 2012, *http://www.justice.gov/defendingchildhood/cev-rpt-full.pdf*. Full quote: "For us in Rosebud, our reservation, the question is not who has been exposed to violence, it's who hasn't been exposed to violence."

[10] Dolores Subia BigFoot et al., "Trauma Exposure in American Indian/Alaska Native Children," Indian Country Child Trauma Center: 1–4 (2008), available at: *http://www.theannainstitute.org/American%20Indians%20and%20Alaska%20Natives/Trauma%20Exposure%20in%20AIAN%20Children.pdf*

[11] Deters, P. B., Novins, D. K., Fickenscher, A., & Beals, J. (2006). Trauma and posttraumatic stress disorder symptomatology: Patterns among AI/AN adolescents in substance abuse treatment. American Journal of Orthopsychiatry, 76(3), 335–345.

proved devastating to tribal communities. The testimony of the witnesses at the hearings underscored the fact that Native Americans share a history of displacement, forced assimilation, and cultural suppression, factors that may contribute to child maltreatment.

Despite the epidemic levels of violence American Indian and Alaska Native children are exposed to, the Advisory Committee discovered that some tribes and urban Indian organizations have found ways to incorporate tradition and develop resources to protect their children from harm and help them heal. The Advisory Committee repeatedly heard testimony indicating that programs for tribal children and youth, including treatment and intervention programs, are most successful if they are based on tribal customs, language, and spiritual ceremonies that are deeply respectful of the traditional cultural values of the child, family and tribe. [12]

The Advisory Committee heard that integration of traditional healing practices into mental health prevention and treatment for Native children and youth is essential. Many of those who testified recognized that, for American Indian and Alaska Native children and their families, emotional and psychological well-being cannot be separated from spiritual well-being. There is growing evidence that Native youth who are culturally and spiritually engaged are more resilient than their peers. [13] For example, research has revealed that over one third of Native adolescents and half of Native adults prefer to seek mental health services from a cultural or spiritual healer. [14] In other research, American Indian caregivers preferred cultural treatments for their children and found the traditionally based ceremonies more effective than standard or typical behavioral health treatment. [15]

OJJDP-Funded Efforts

In 2010, the Department of Justice launched its Coordinated Tribal Assistance Solicitation (CTAS) in direct response to tribes seeking a more streamlined, comprehensive grant process. CTAS gives tribes the flexibility needed to better address their criminal justice and public safety needs.

In Fiscal Year 2014, the Department awarded CTAS grants to 169 American Indian tribes, Alaska Native villages, tribal consortia and tribal designees. The grants provide more than $87 million to enhance law enforcement practices and sustain crime prevention and intervention efforts in nine purpose areas including public safety and community policing; justice systems planning; alcohol and substance abuse; corrections and correctional alternatives; violence against women; juvenile justice; and tribal youth programs.

As a part of the Attorney General's Defending Childhood Initiative, OJJDP funded two initiatives that are tribally-directed and sensitive to tribal traditions and culture. The Rosebud Sioux Tribe in South Dakota delivers trauma-informed services, rooted in Lakota values that address educational, justice system, and health-care needs. The Chippewa Cree Tribe at the Rocky Boy reservation in Montana is involving elders and youth from throughout the community in the design of prevention and treatment programs that rely on traditional health and healing methods. These are promising approaches that take into account tribal customs aimed at enhancing resilience in affected children, and they represent some of the exciting work already being done to support children in tribal communities. Recently, leaders from both tribes participated in a three-day training on indigenous treatment for trauma offered by the National Native Child Trauma Center.

---

[12] "One of the main barriers both our youth and their families face are professionals who have the proper credentials required by the state but lack the cultural knowledge and ability or desire to even try to understand where our children and their families are coming from." Darla Thiele, Director, Sunka Wakan Ah Ku Program Testimony before the Task Force on American Indian/Alaska Native Children Exposed to Violence Hearing in Bismarck, ND, December 9, 2014

[13] Gone, J.P., & Alcantara, C., "Identifying Effective Mental Health Interventions for American Indians and Alaska Natives: A Review of the Literature," *Cultural Diversity and Ethnic minority Psychology*, 13(4), (2007): 356–363.

[14] Grey, N., & Nye P. S., "American Indian and Alaska Native Substance Abuse: Co-Morbidity and Cultural Issues," American Indian and Alaska Native Mental Health Research, 10(2), (2001): 67–82.; Rieckmann, T. R., Wadsworth, M. E., & Deyhle, D., "Cultural Identity, Explanatory Style, and Depression in Navajo Adolescents," Cultural Diversity & Ethnic Minority Psychology, 10(4), (2004): 365–382.; Spicer, P., Novins, D. K., Mitchell, C. M., & Beals, J., "Aboriginal Social Organization, Contemporary Experience and American Indian Adolescent Alcohol Use," Quarterly Journal of Studies on Alcohol, 64(4), (2003): 450–457.; Yoder, K. A., Whitbeck, L. B., Hoyt, D. R., & LaFromboise, T., "Suicide Ideation Among American Indian Youths," Archives of Suicide Research, 10(2).(2006): 177–190.

[15] Walls, M. L., Johnson, K. D., Whitbeck, L. B., & Hoyt, D. R., "Mental Health and Substance Abuse Services Preferences Among American Indian People of the Northern Midwest," Community Mental Health Journal, 42(6), (2006): 521–535.

OJJDP is funding efforts to enhance the capacity of Tribal Healing to Wellness Courts to respond to alcohol-related issues of tribal youth who are younger than 21. A Tribal Healing to Wellness Court is not simply a tribal criminal or family court that orders individuals to treatment. Rather, it is an innovative and collaborative legal process that adapts the drug court concept and its key components to meet the need of referred youth in a manner that respects and includes tribal traditions. Under this initiative, participating courts are developing or enhancing policy, procedure, assessment tools, or service models that address underage drinking. A second component of the initiative will deliver training and technical assistance to the participating tribal courts. All programming is based on the 10 Key Components of an effective Tribal Healing to Wellness Courts, modeled after policies developed by the National Association of Drug Court Professionals. Current funding supports five tribes—Yurok Tribe (CA), Lac Du Flambeau Tribe of Lake Superior Chippewa Indians (WI), Southern Ute Indian Tribe (CO), White Earth Nation (MN), Winnebago Tribe of Nebraska (NE)—and a training and technical assistance provider. This program will be expanded in Fiscal Year 2015 to support additional tribes.

Reaching children and families in tribal communities is a priority for the National Center for Missing & Exploited Children (NCMEC). NCMEC, which is funded by OJJDP, operates a national toll-free hotline and serves as a clearinghouse and resource center that collects and distributes data regarding missing and exploited children. NCMEC collaborates with tribal leaders and communities to address pressing issues such as multi-generational intra-familial sexual abuse, heavy substance abuse across generations, and the sexual exploitation of women and children. NCMEC is developing closer working relationships with tribal communities and organizations to help identify and provide resources and services to children and families living on tribal lands. In 2014, NCMEC added a Tribal Law Enforcement Liaison to its staff to help enhance collaboration with tribal law enforcement agencies; hosted a Tribal Cultural Awareness training for staff; and worked with tribal communities, schools and law enforcement to offer training.

Efforts like these, as well as OJJDP funding that goes towards child advocacy centers, Internet Crimes Against Children (ICAC) task forces, and our youth tribal portfolio, are important ways OJJDP is working to prevent and address trauma in American Indian and Alaskan Native communities and tribes.

Research

OJP's National Institute of Justice (NIJ), in partnership with OJJDP and OJP's Office for Victims of Crime (OVC), is funding a 30-month study intended to improve the health and well-being of youth in American Indian and Alaska Native communities who may have been exposed to violence and victimization. The study will develop and test a survey instrument and different administration modes that can effectively assess exposure to violence and victimization and determine the feasibility of using these procedures in tribal communities and settings. Although some research suggests higher rates of violence in tribal communities, there has never been a national study of tribal youth regarding their victimization experiences that provides reliable, valid estimates of the scope of the problem. As a result, the exact incidence, prevalence, and nature of victimization experienced by youth living in tribal communities requires more research.

As part of the Attorney General's Children Exposed to Violence Demonstration Program, NIJ has funded evaluations in two tribal communities (i.e., Chippewa Cree and Rosebud Sioux Tribes) that include a community survey addressing children's exposure to violence as well as knowledge of and attitudes towards children's exposure to violence and the prevalence of violence. Findings from these evaluations will highlight the models used by Tribal Nations to prevent, treat, and raise awareness about children's exposure to violence, emphasizing the role of culture; discuss local challenges with implementing programs to address children's exposure to violence; and provide recommendations for other communities looking to prevent, treat, and raise awareness about children's exposure to violence.

Responding to Victims

OVC is engaged in several initiatives in Indian Country. OVC has responded to the challenge of helping service providers meet the needs of drug-endangered youth in American Indian and Alaska Native communities by producing a video series entitled, ''A Circle of Healing for Native Children Endangered by Drugs.'' This series not only explains the role that historical trauma has played in generating the complex traumatic stress experienced by these children, but it also highlights ongoing efforts to integrate cultural practices and traditional healing into therapeutic interventions for American Indian and Alaska Native families struggling with addiction and child maltreatment issues. OVC will debut the video at its upcoming Indian Nations Conference in December and is confident that it will become an invaluable tool in helping child welfare and mental health professionals, among others, who are seeking information on innovative techniques to improve outcomes for drug-endangered children in American Indian and Alaska Native communities.

OVC funds the Children's Justice Act (CJA) Partnerships for Indian Communities Grant Program. OVC dedicated $8.1 million to support tribes in developing, establishing and operating programs to improve the investigation, prosecution and handling of child abuse cases, particularly cases of child sexual abuse, in a manner that limits additional trauma to child victims. The funding further supports the development and implementation of comprehensive programs for abused children, and procedures to address child abuse cases in tribal courts and child protection service systems. OVC is also working with the Flandreau Indian School, a Bureau of Indian Education boarding school in South Dakota, to provide specialized mental health services to students identified as victims. OVC is providing $1.5 million to support this demonstration project with the goal of establishing a culturally appropriate, trauma-informed system of care for students with long-term exposure to violence, trauma, and victimization.

Closing Statement

Mr. Chairman, OJJDP strives to strengthen the juvenile justice system's efforts to protect public safety, hold offenders accountable and provide services that address the needs of youth and their families. We are committed to working with American Indian and Alaskan Native communities, and our partner agencies within the Department of Justice and throughout federal and state governments, to implement evidence-based approaches to preventing and addressing child trauma. I appreciate the opportunity to appear before you today, and I am prepared to respond to any questions you may have.

The CHAIRMAN. Thank you very much, Mr. Listenbee
Yvette Roubideaux.

STATEMENT OF HON. YVETTE ROUBIDEAUX, MD, MPH, ACTING DIRECTOR, INDIAN HEALTH SERVICE

Dr. ROUBIDEAUX. Thank you, Mr. Chairman, Vice Chairman Barrasso, and members of the Committee.

I am Dr. Yvette Roubideaux, Acting Director of the Indian Health Service. I appreciate the opportunity to testify on preventing and addressing childhood trauma in Indian Country.

Thank you so much for holding this hearing today on such a truly important topic. It is a serious problem with multiple reasons and causes as detailed in the testimony and has a profound impact on our communities.

The problem of childhood trauma is multigenerational and a societal problem. It is sweeping in scope and will take a coordinated, comprehensive, multidimensional, public health response to change the course for our children and youth.

I appreciate the opportunity discuss with the Committee what IHS is doing to address the many issues related to childhood trauma and be a part of the solution for these public health challenges.

IHS is already and wants to continue to be a partner with other agencies, stakeholders and tribes in these efforts to find solutions. My testimony summarizes some of the major national programs and activities that IHS does for this issue as a part of our medical and public health response to childhood trauma.

For the sake of time, I will just summarize by saying that the IHS' policies, training, programs and partnerships promote a multifaceted range of activities for the identification, treatment and prevention of childhood trauma.

However, IHS cannot address these issues alone and it will take all of us to prevent and reduce childhood trauma. We welcome your partnership and assistance with this important issue.

That concludes my remarks. Thank you.

[The prepared statement of Dr. Roubideaux follows:]

PREPARED STATEMENT OF HON. YVETTE ROUBIDEAUX, MD, MPH, ACTING DIRECTOR, INDIAN HEALTH SERVICE

Mr. Chairman and Members of the Committee:

Good afternoon, I am Dr. Yvette Roubideaux, Acting Director of the Indian Health Service (IHS). Today, I appreciate the opportunity to testify on preventing and addressing childhood trauma in Indian Country.

Background

As you know, the IHS plays a unique role in the U.S. Department of Health and Human Services (HHS) to meet the federal trust responsibility to provide health care to American Indian and Alaska Native (AI/AN) people. The IHS provides comprehensive health service delivery to 2.1 million American Indians and Alaska Natives through a system of IHS, Tribal, and urban Indian operated facilities and programs based on treaties, judicial determinations, and Acts of Congress. The mission of the agency is to raise the physical, mental, social, and spiritual health of AI/AN people to the highest level, in partnership with the population we serve. The agency aims to assure that comprehensive, culturally acceptable personal and public health services are available and accessible to the service population. Our foundation is to promote healthy AI/AN people, communities, and cultures, and to honor the inherent sovereign rights of Tribes.

Two major pieces of legislation are at the core of the Federal Government's responsibility for meeting the health needs of American Indians and Alaska Natives: The Snyder Act of 1921, P.L. 67–85, and the Indian Health Care Improvement Act (IHCIA), P.L. 94–437, as amended. The Snyder Act authorized appropriations for "the relief of distress and conservation of health" of American Indians and Alaska Natives. The IHCIA was enacted "to implement the federal responsibility for the care of the Indian people by improving the services and facilities of federal Indian health programs and encouraging maximum participation of Indians in such programs." Like the Snyder Act, the IHCIA provides the authority for the provision of programs, services, functions and activities to address the health needs of American Indians and Alaska Natives. The IHCIA includes authorities for the recruitment and retention of health professionals serving Indian communities, health services for AI/AN people, and the construction, replacement, and repair of healthcare facilities, among other authorities.

The IHS, in partnership with Tribes and urban Indian health programs, provides essential medical and mental health services in over 600 hospitals, clinics, and health stations. These services include medical and surgical inpatient care, emergency care, ambulatory care, mental health and substance abuse treatment and prevention, and medical support services such as laboratory, pharmacy, nutrition, diagnostic imaging, medical records, and physical therapy. Other services include public and community health programs such as diabetes; maternal and child health; communicable diseases such as influenza, HIV/AIDS, tuberculosis, and hepatitis; suicide prevention; substance abuse prevention; women's and elders' health; domestic violence prevention and treatment; and regional trauma/emergency medical delivery systems. The level of services provided in each community varies based on available resources. In addition, over half of the IHS budget is managed by Tribes under P.L. 93–638, the Indian Self Determination and Educational Assistance Act, and many of the public, community and behavioral health programs are managed by Tribes even when the hospital or clinic is still under management by the IHS.

Childhood Trauma in AI/AN Children

According to the National Child Abuse and Neglect Data System, an estimated 686,000 children were exposed to incidents of child abuse and neglect in 2012. These data translate to a rate of 9.2 occurrences of child abuse and neglect for every 1,000 children per year.[1] While these data are not unique to AI/AN children, childhood

[1] U.S. Department of Health & Human Services. Administration for Children and Families. (2012). Child Maltreatment 2012. Available at *http://www.acf.hss.gov/programs/cb/stats*lresearch/index.htm#can

trauma is disproportionately experienced by AI/AN children. The reasons are multi-factorial and related to the high incidence of alcohol and drug abuse, mental health disorders, suicide, violence, and behaviorally-related chronic diseases among AI/AN people. Recurrent physical, emotional, and sexual abuse, as well as emotional and physical neglect leads to childhood trauma impacting the mental health and wellbeing of children. Other contributing factors of childhood trauma include household members who may have a substance abuse disorder, chronic depression, or other mental health diagnoses, family members who may be incarcerated, experience suicidal ideation, domestic violence in the household, and parental loss. Each of these serious behavioral health related issues have a profound impact on childhood trauma, the health of individuals, family, and community wellbeing.

Once again, another school shooting has shaken us to our core as one of the Nation's most serious tragedies. The heartbreak facing the Marysville, Washington, community and Tulalip Tribe offers another opportunity for a collective effort to reduce the chances of similar future tragedies. There are no easy solutions and no single agency or single approach that will address the violence and many other problems impacting the mental health of our children and youth. The problem of childhood trauma is a multigenerational and societal problem. It is sweeping in scope and will take a coordinated, comprehensive, multi-dimensional public health response to change the course for our children and youth. Today, I appreciate the opportunity to discuss what the IHS is doing to address the many issues that relate to childhood trauma and to be part of the solution for these public health challenges. IHS is already, and wants to continue to be, a partner with other agencies, stakeholders and Tribes in these efforts to find solutions.

IHS Medical and Public Health Response to Childhood Trauma

The overall structure and types of services provided by IHS, Tribal and urban Indian health programs were described above. The funding IHS receives to provide primary care and behavioral health services is through the Hospitals and Health Clinics, Mental Health and Alcohol and Substance Abuse budgets, of which over 50 percent of funds are transferred under P.L. 93–638 contracts or compacts to Tribal governments or Tribal organizations that design and manage the delivery of health programs in their communities. In addition, there are 34 urban Indian health programs serving approximately 600,000 AI/AN people, including children with varying levels of services.

In Fiscal Year (FY) 2013, IHS per capita spending estimates were $47 per person for mental health services and $117 per person for alcohol and substance abuse services. The average public and private expenditure among school-age American children from 2009–2011 was $2,192 for mental health services.[2] While the IHS overall spending estimate on mental health services is not directly comparable for the amount spent per AI/AN child due to the nature of how services are accessed through our health system, it is a glimpse into the complexities faced by Tribes in providing comprehensive services for children and families. I would like to provide an overview of some of our major national programs and activities that are part of the IHS medical and public health response to childhood trauma.

National Policy

I spoke in my introduction about the dire statistics on child abuse and neglect and its huge impact on AI/AN children and youth. IHS works to positively influence the outcomes for children and youth who are victims of child maltreatment through development of policies, objectives, procedures, and responsibilities concerning the detection, management, prevention, and evaluation of child abuse and neglect. The IHS recently recognized the need for a more comprehensive, standalone policy, and the IHS is drafting a comprehensive national Child Maltreatment policy to ensure children who are abused or neglected receive comprehensive intervention and treatment services when they enter our health system, as well as outlines the health care responsibilities in providing a coordinated multidisciplinary response. This policy will help improve and enhance our overall response at IHS facilities.

Training

The IHS offers a comprehensive training program to meet the needs of our workforce as it relates to addressing childhood trauma. Specific for child abuse, IHS provides training related to the identification, collection, and preservation of medical forensic evidence obtained during the treatment of child sexual abuse. Monthly

---

[2] U.S. Department of Health & Human Services., (2014). Expenditures for Treatment of Mental Health Disorders among Children, Ages 5–17, 2009–2011: Estimates for U.S. Civilian Non-institutionalized Population. Published by Agency for Healthcare Research and Quality. Available at: *http://meps.ahrq.gov/mepsweb/data*lfiles/publications/st440/stat440.shtml

webinars ensure the Indian health system receives the continuing education needed to maintain competencies in the treatment, prevention, and coordination of services for child maltreatment. For current and pressing behavioral health issues related to childhood trauma, the IHS provides virtual training seminars and consultation sessions on topics including child mental health, childhood trauma, suicide, historical trauma, Fetal Alcohol Spectrum Disorders, and school violence, among others.

Youth Regional Treatment Centers

To help youth battling substance abuse, IHS administers ten Youth Regional Treatment Centers (YRTCs) that provide inpatient treatment for substance abuse and co-occurring mental health disorders among AI/AN youth. The YRTCs provide a range of clinical services rooted in culturally relevant, holistic models of care including group, individual, and family psychotherapy, life skills development, medication management, aftercare relapse prevention, and post-treatment follow up services. YRTCs also provide education, culture-based prevention activities, and evidence- and practice-based models of treatment to assist youth overcome their challenges and become healthy, strong, and resilient community members.

Recently, the Jack Brown Center, an IHS funded YRTC that is located in Tahlequah, Oklahoma, completed construction on a new facility that will increase Jack Brown's capacity from 20 to 36 inpatient beds. Additionally, Congress authorized two YRTCs to be built in the IHS California Area. The Southern California facility is expected to open in FY 2015, and staffing costs were included in the FY 2015 President's Budget. The FY 2015 Budget also included construction costs for the Northern California YRTC.

Community Health Representatives

The IHS Community Health Representative, or CHR, program is community-based program with a special focus on advocacy, health promotion, and disease prevention. In 2013, the CHR program partnered with Johns Hopkins University to implement Family Spirit, an evidence-based and culturally tailored in-home parent training and support program. Parents gain knowledge and skills to achieve optimum development for their preschool aged children across the domains of physical, cognitive, social-emotional, language learning, and self-help. The program is currently the largest, most rigorous, and only evidence-based home visiting program ever designed specifically for American Indian families. In 2013, IHS provided funding to further replicate the program in three American Indian communities.

Methamphetamine and Suicide Prevention Initiative

The IHS Methamphetamine and Suicide Prevention Initiative, or MSPI, is one of the most significant efforts at the core of the IHS' response to methamphetamine abuse and suicide in AI/AN communities. The MSPI's purpose is to promote the use and development of evidence-based and practice-based models that represent culturally-appropriate prevention and treatment approaches to methamphetamine abuse and suicide prevention from a community-driven context. Of the 130 IHS, Tribal, and urban Indian health projects supported across the country through the MSPI, over 80 percent of projects provide prevention and treatment services to youth. For example, one Tribal project increased access to services by funding school based mental health professionals at community schools. Youth now have immediate access to mental health providers in a familiar environment. These professionals are responsible for providing on-going mental health services to youth, as well as providing educational groups related to suicide, grief, and loss. School officials have witnessed the impact of the school-based health services and report youth are more likely to talk about suicide and reach out for help.

Throughout the 5 years of the MSPI, projects have significantly raised awareness through diverse and innovative programming. From 2009–2013, the MSPI resulted in more than 7,500 individuals entering treatment for methamphetamine abuse, over 15,000 tele-health substance abuse and mental health encounters, over 10,000 professionals and community members trained in suicide prevention and crisis response, and over 400,000 encounters with youth were provided as part of evidence-based and practice-based intervention and prevention services.

Community Awareness

To raise youth awareness on the issues of substance abuse and suicide, the IHS partnered with the Northwest Portland Area Indian Health Board to develop media campaigns. Using focus groups, youth developed the "I Strengthen My Nation" and "Community is the Healer" media campaigns, which empower Native youth to resist drugs and alcohol, motivates parents to talk openly to their children about drug and alcohol use, and raises awareness about the issue of suicide.

Domestic Violence Prevention Initiative

To prevent domestic and sexual violence, as well as family violence, the IHS administers the Domestic Violence Prevention Initiative, or DVPI. Through DVPI, 65 IHS, Tribal, and urban Indian health projects provide outreach, victim advocacy, intervention, policy development, and community response teams. From 2010–2012, the DVPI resulted in over 28,000 direct service encounters including crisis intervention, victim advocacy, case management, and counseling services; over 36,000 referrals for domestic violence services, culturally-based services, and clinical behavioral health services; with 487 forensic evidence collection kits submitted to federal, state, and Tribal law enforcement.

Drug and Alcohol Exposure during Pregnancy

To identify women who are using alcohol and drugs during pregnancy, IHS healthcare facilities conduct screening during routine women's health and prenatal encounters. In FY 2013, 65.7 percent of all AI/AN females ages 15 to 44 were screened for alcohol use. In one IHS service unit, approximately 54 percent of women tested positive for drug use while pregnant and 52 percent of the infants born tested positive for drugs. To combat this problem, IHS has drafted policies and coordinated efforts for a comprehensive and multidisciplinary response to provide services to mothers and families including prenatal services, treatment, and home visiting programs to promote healthy lifestyles.

Fetal Alcohol Spectrum Disorder

For the babies born with Fetal Alcohol Spectrum Disorders, or FASD, which is an umbrella term describing the range of effects that can occur in an individual whose mother drank alcohol during pregnancy, IHS administers the Fetal Alcohol and Drug Unit (Unit), located within the University of Washington's Alcohol and Drug Abuse Institute. The Unit provides FASD information and strategies for prevention and intervention to AI/AN communities. Since 2012, over 300 high-risk, substance-abusing pregnant and parenting women and their families have received evaluation, diagnosis, and referral services through the Unit. Additionally, the Unit has provided training and technical assistance to over 4,400 healthcare providers and AI/AN community members on FASD prevention and intervention topics.

IHS Partnerships

The IHS has devoted considerable effort to develop and share effective programs throughout the Indian health system. Strategies to address public safety and justice issues that impact childhood trauma include collaborations and partnerships between IHS, Substance Abuse and Mental Health Services Administration, Department of Justice (DOJ), and Department of Interior (DOI) through three Memoranda of Understanding, established by the Tribal Law and Order Act, Indian Health Care Improvement Act, and Individuals with Disabilities Education Act. These interagency coordination efforts work to ensure Federal agencies are comprehensively addressing the serious problems that have a significant impact on childhood trauma, such as alcohol, substance abuse, mental illness.

The IHS is working with other federal officials from DOJ and DOI as part of the Defending Childhood Initiative as a member of the American Indian/Alaska Native Children Exposed to Violence Federal workgroup. This partnership seeks to take immediate steps to improve the Federal response to AI/AN children exposed to violence. The role of IHS in this group is to ensure services are comprehensive and coordinated so that every child has access to medical and counseling appointments in a timely manner and on a routine basis.

The IHS partnership with the American Academy of Pediatrics' Committee on Native American Child Health (CONACH) works to develop policies and programs to improve the health of AI/AN children. CONACH members are committed to increasing awareness of the major health problems facing Native American children and monitoring legislation affecting AI/AN child health. CONACH conducts pediatric consultation visits to IHS and Tribal healthcare facilities, makes recommendations to improve services, and works to strengthen ties with Tribes throughout the United States.

Summary

In summary, IHS policies, training, programs, and partnerships promote a multi-faceted range of activities for identification, treatment and prevention of childhood trauma. However, IHS cannot address this issue alone, and it is imperative to continue to build a wide safety net of Federal, non-Federal and Tribal resources for AI/AN children and families to help to further activities at the national, Tribal, state, and local levels. No one individual, community, or agency can do this alone. It will take all of us to prevent and reduce childhood trauma and we welcome your partnership and assistance with this important issue.

This concludes my remarks and I welcome any questions that you may have. Thank you.

The CHAIRMAN. Thank you, Dr. Roubideaux.

Kana.

STATEMENT OF KANA ENOMOTO, PRINCIPAL DEPUTY ADMINISTRATOR, SUBSTANCE ABUSE AND MENTAL HEALTH SERVICES ADMINISTRATION

Ms. ENOMOTO. Good afternoon, Chairman Tester, Vice Chairman Barrasso and members of the Committee.

Thank you for inviting the Substance Abuse and Mental Health Services Administration to testify here today. I am pleased to be here with my colleagues from IHS, DOJ and from the field.

I am particularly pleased to be here this morning, Senator Heitkamp, because I too heard from the faces of the statistics. SAMHSA's Native Youth Conference was convened and we had a Federal listening panel.

We heard loudly and clearly from Native youth from across the country that they want us to address childhood trauma. They want us to address the violence and the substance abuse in their communities and they want to be our partners in finding ways to heal and help their communities find a path to recovery, to hope and wellness, and doing that in a culturally, developmentally appropriate way.

SAMHSA has many programs in its portfolio that address this issue. You also have that in my written testimony. I want to highlight for you one particular program; The Tribal Behavioral Health Grant Program.

The President has requested for several years in a row funding to provide stable, predictable funding to all tribes to do substance abuse prevention, suicide prevention and mental health promotion in ways that fit their needs, that they can determine the best practices to use in that space.

Just this last year, in FY14, Congress started us off with $5 million and we were able to give grants to 20 tribes with some of the highest rates of suicide. As you can imagine, that is not enough.

We need to do more and look forward to doing more. We have invested for many years in the National Child Traumatic Stress Initiative which Dr. van den Pol will tell you more about. That is a space where we are also trying to promote effective clinical interventions for child trauma. We have funded the center at the University of Montana where we can bring together effective clinical interventions with cultural adaptations and traditional healing practices.

We hope to do much more of that and partner with our colleagues across the Federal Government and Indian Country.

We thank you very much for having this hearing.

[The prepared statement of Ms. Enomoto follows:]

PREPARED STATEMENT OF KANA ENOMOTO, PRINCIPAL DEPUTY ADMINISTRATOR, SUBSTANCE ABUSE AND MENTAL HEALTH SERVICES ADMINISTRATION

Chairman Tester, Ranking Member Barrasso, and members of the Senate Committee on Indian Affairs, thank you for inviting me to testify at this important hearing on protecting our children's mental health. I am pleased to testify along with my colleagues from the Indian Health Service (IHS) and the Department of Justice, and inform the Committee of the Administration's efforts to prevent and address childhood trauma in Indian Country. I am particularly pleased to be here today for several reasons. First, I began my career at the Substance Abuse and Mental Health Services Administration (SAMHSA) over fourteen years ago working on childhood trauma programs and have had the opportunity to see the agency's programs evolve and expand over the years. In addition, just this past summer I accompanied Administrator Hyde to Indian Country where we visited tribes and Alaska Native villages in three of the states represented by members of this Committee. Shortly thereafter, SAMHSA established the agency's Office of Tribal Affairs and Policy (OTAP), which serves as SAMHSA's primary point of contact for tribal governments, tribal organizations, Federal departments and agencies' tribal affairs efforts, and other governments and agencies on behavioral health issues facing American Indian and Alaska Native (AI/AN) populations in the United States. Finally, as I speak, SAMHSA is wrapping up its 2014 Native Youth Conference, which has focused on addressing behavioral health issues facing AI/AN youth.

SAMHSA

As you are aware, SAMHSA's mission is to reduce the impact of substance abuse and mental illness on America's communities. SAMHSA envisions a Nation that acts on the knowledge that:

- Behavioral health is essential for health;
- Prevention works;
- Treatment is effective; and
- People recover from mental and substance use disorders.

In order to achieve this mission, SAMHSA has identified six Strategic Initiatives to focus the Agency's work on improving lives and capitalizing on emerging opportunities. SAMHSA's top Strategic Initiatives are: Prevention of Substance Abuse and Mental Illness; Health Care and Health Systems Integration; Trauma and Justice; Recovery Support; Health Information Technology; and Workforce Development.

SAMHSA's Trauma and Justice Strategic Initiative provides a comprehensive public health approach to addressing trauma and establishing a trauma-informed approach in health, behavioral health, human services, and related systems, with the intent to reduce both the observable and less visible harmful effects of trauma and violence on children and youth, adults, families, and communities. Recent activities of the strategic initiative include hosting a Tribal Juvenile Justice Policy Academy and releasing SAMHSA's paper entitled "Concept of Trauma and Guidance for a Trauma-Informed Approach." SAMHSA has participated in the Department of Justice's Task Force on American Indian and Alaska Native Children Exposed to Violence and will work with our partners at the Office of Juvenile Justice and Delinquency Prevention to address the recommendations of the report.

The Concept of Trauma and Guidance for a Trauma-Informed Approach publication was released in July of this year. SAMHSA intends this framework to be relevant to its Federal partners and their state, tribal and local system counterparts and applicable to practitioners, researchers, and trauma survivors, families and communities. The framework is anchored in SAMHSA's concept of trauma which is that "individual trauma results from an event, series of events, or set of circumstances that is experienced by an individual as physically or emotionally harmful or life threatening and that has lasting adverse effects on the individual's functioning, and mental, physical, social, emotional or spiritual well-being."[1] The focus on experience highlights the fact that not every child will experience the same events as traumatic. While the immediate focus might be on a recent event, the individual's reaction to that event may be affected by earlier experiences. As an example: A child bullied in school that comes for treatment or support may have experienced neglect or abuse at home, lived in multiple foster care settings, and witnessed the impact of community violence. That child may experience the bullying event

---

[1] Substance Abuse and Mental Health Services Administration. *SAMHSA's Concept of Trauma and Guidance for a Trauma-Informed Approach.* HHS Publication No. (SMA) 14–4884. Rockville, MD: Substance Abuse and Mental Health Services Administration, 2014.

very differently from a child who has not been exposed to prior traumatic events or circumstances.

Prevalence of Behavioral Health Conditions and Treatment

According to SAMHSA's 2012 National Survey on Drug Use and Health (NSDUH), the statistics related to behavioral health conditions among the AI/populations are very troubling.

Mental Health

- 5.2 percent of American Indian/Alaska Native youth had a major depressive episode (MDE) and 2.6 percent had an MDE with severe impairment.
- NSDUH also found that in 2012, 11 percent of AI/AN youth had specialty mental health services during the past year with services provided in a range of settings from education and juvenile justice settings to general and specialty health settings.

Substance Misuse and Abuse

- The rate of substance dependence or abuse among people aged 12 and up was higher among the AI/AN population (21.8 percent) than among other groups.
- AI/AN individuals have the highest rate of binge alcohol use (30.2 percent) compared with other groups.
- American Indians and Alaska Natives are also more likely than other groups in the United States to die from drug-induced deaths, according to a 2013 Centers for Disease Control and Prevention (CDC) report on U.S. health disparities and inequities.

Suicidal Thoughts, Attempts and Completions

Based on data from SAMHSA and CDC, we also know that AI/AN youth are disproportionally impacted by suicide.

- In 2011, American Indian and Alaska Native high school students reported rates of suicide attempts nearly twice that of the general population of U.S. high school students (14.7 percent vs. 7.8 percent).
- In 2012, the suicide rate among American Indians and Alaska Natives ages 10 to 24 years was 14.2 per 100,000, significantly higher than the suicide rate for people of the same age with the next highest rate (white 8.66) and almost three times the suicide rate for Asian/Pacific Islanders (5.51) and blacks (5.27).
- In 2012, 5.9 percent of American Indians and Alaska Natives ages 18 and up had serious thoughts of suicide in the past year. This is higher than any other single racial or ethnic group.

Trauma

Based on SAMHSA's definition of trauma, the agency is in the process of developing and implementing trauma measures for population surveillance, client level data, facilities surveys, and quality measures.

Improving Practice

SAMHSA, as the Federal agency that leads public health efforts to advance the behavioral health of the nation, has several roles. I just spoke about the ways in which SAMHSA provides leadership and voice and supports the behavioral health field with critical data from national surveys and surveillance. SAMHSA also has a vital role in collecting best practices and developing expertise around prevention and treatment for people with mental illness and substance use disorders. SAMHSA's staff includes subject matter experts that provide technical assistance and training to individuals, organizations, states, tribes, and others every day. SAMHSA also supports a number of technical assistance and training centers that are focused on children's mental health and addressing and preventing trauma.

The SAMHSA Tribal Training and Technical Assistance (TTA) Center uses a culturally relevant, evidence-based, holistic approach to support Native communities in their self-determination efforts through infrastructure development and capacity building, as well as program planning and implementation. It provides training and technical assistance on mental and/or substance use disorders, suicide prevention, and mental health promotion. It also offers training and technical assistance, ranging from broad to focused and intense to federally recognized tribes, SAMHSA tribal grantees, and tribal organizations serving Indian Country.

The National Center for Child Traumatic Stress (NCCTS) facilitates collaborative activity, oversees resource development, and coordinates national training and education for the National Child Traumatic Stress Network. Housed jointly at the UCLA Neuropsychiatric Institute and the Duke University Medical Center, the NCCTS works to increase access to services and raise the standard of care for traumatized children and their families.

The Suicide Prevention Resource Center (SPRC) also has a special focus on American Indians and Alaska Natives. SPRC provides technical assistance, training, and materials to increase the knowledge and expertise of suicide prevention practitioners and other professionals serving people at risk for suicide.

SAMHSA has also published ''To Live To See the Great Day That Dawns: Preventing Suicide by American Indian and Alaska Native Youth and Young Adults'' which lays the groundwork for community-based suicide prevention and mental health promotion plans for American Indian and Alaska Native youth and young adults.

Public Awareness and Support

Creating public awareness of children's mental health issues and targeting campaigns to prevent and address childhood trauma is a key role that SAMHSA plays in reducing the impact of mental illness and substance abuse in America's communities. For example, in 2006 the SAMHSA-funded National Suicide Prevention Lifeline created a specific set of outreach materials for AI/AN teen suicide prevention public awareness campaign. The poster utilized in the campaign depicts an American Indian male who appears to have lost hope. But, the image emphasizes that there is help, and with help comes hope and urges those who are thinking about suicide to call the Lifeline. Posters to promote AI/AN use of the Lifeline are available for free from SAMHSA's website and can be downloaded and printed or ordered from SAMHSA's online store. SAMHSA encourages tribes and tribal organization to place the posters in a wide range of settings to ensure AI/AN individuals are aware of the Lifeline.

As part of SAMHSA's highly successful ''Talk. They Hear You.'' underage drinking prevention campaign, a promotion video was recently recorded with Rod Robinson, the former Director of SAMHSA's Office of Indian Alcohol and Substance Abuse. In the video Mr. Robinson discusses materials developed to help prevent and reduce underage drinking in American Indian communities and he responds to questions such as why underage drinking is an important concern for American Indian populations. He also communicates ways in which the new ''Talk. They Hear You.'' materials will help parents and adult caregivers address underage drinking within tribal communities. The video is available on SAMHSA's You Tube channel.

Strategic Grant Making

National Child Traumatic Stress Initiative

Established in 2000, the purpose of the National Child Traumatic Stress Initiative (NCTSI) is to improve behavioral health treatment, services, and interventions for children and adolescents exposed to traumatic events. It has done so through the National Child Traumatic Stress Network (NCSTN), a national network of centers with expertise in child trauma. The goals of the NCTSN are to develop highly effective clinical and service interventions for child trauma, expand availability and accessibility of effective trauma-informed interventions, and promote better understanding of issues relevant to developing and providing effective interventions for children, adolescents, and families exposed to traumatic events. To date, the NCTSI has funded over 200 grants across the country.

The National Native Children's Trauma Center (NNCTC) at the University of Montana works in collaboration with IHS and other providers in tribal communities across the country to utilize evidence-based, culturally appropriate, trauma-informed interventions for AI/AN children, youth, and families who experience disproportionate violence, grief, and/or poverty; and childhood, historical, and/or intergenerational trauma. The NNCTC has delivered education and services in a broad range of locations and settings including the Fort Peck, Rocky Boy, Northern Cheyenne, Crow, Pine Ridge, White Earth, Leech Lake, Blackfeet and Flathead Reservations; Cracking Ice Lake, Pine Point, and Waubun, Minnesota; and Bethel, Anchorage, Emmonak, and Napis, Alaska just to name a few. NNCTC provides trainings and consultation in trauma-focused interventions such as Trauma-Focused Cognitive Behavioral Therapy; Attachment, Self-Regulation and Competency Clinical Services; Family Engagement through the Joining Process: Welcome, Honor, and Connect; trauma awareness, implications of the Adverse Childhood Experiences study; and the Students, Trauma, and Resiliency curriculum. The NNCTC has trained social workers, school counselors, nurses, and child protection workers. From April to June 2014, the NNCTC trained 1,180 individuals provided services at 46 sites and collaborated with 58 other organizations.

Other tribal focused grantees include the Native American Health Center (NAH) in Oakland, CA, which is using grant resources to further bridge the gap between western and AI/AN models of addressing trauma.

In the past year, using evidence-based and trauma-focused interventions, NAH therapists have been working with three school age siblings who experienced multiple traumas, including the sudden death of their mother. NAH therapists integrated culturally adapted evidence-based trauma interventions developed and disseminated by the National Child Traumatic Stress Network, with traditional Native healing practices including participation in Cultural Ceremonies. For example, at the start of their treatment, one of the children was at risk for placement in a hospital or residential care setting, and the other two had significant behavior and emotional problems. At present all three are together in the care of their mother's sister and nearing a successful end to their treatment. As a result of the multi-focused trauma treatment and the interventions of therapists, children and families are receiving effective and culturally sensitive healing services.

Tribal Behavioral Health Grants

For several years, the President's Budget for SAMHSA had requested funding to address the high incidence of substance abuse and suicide in AI/AN youth and young adult populations. In Fiscal Year 2014, Congress appropriated for the first time $5 million to begin such a program, Tribal Behavioral Health (Native Connections). SAMHSA recently awarded 20 Tribal Behavioral Health grants of $200,000 to tribes or tribal organizations with high rates of suicide to develop and implement a plan that addresses suicide and substance abuse (including alcohol) and is designed to promote mental health among tribal youth. Grantees such as the Selawik Village Council in Alaska, the Turtle Mountain Band of Chippewa Tribe in North Dakota, and the Pueblo of Nambe in New Mexico, indicated in their applications how they will incorporate evidence-based, culture-based, and practice-based strategies for tribal youth. Grantees are required to work across tribal suicide prevention, mental health, substance abuse prevention, and substance abuse treatment programs to build positive behavioral health among youth. Using real-time surveillance data of suicide deaths and attempts, grantees will create or enhance effective systems of follow up for those identified at risk of suicide and/or substance abuse or mental health issues that could lead to suicide. With a focus on tribal traditions, interagency collaboration, early identification, community healing, and preventing future deaths by suicide, grantees will connect appropriate cultural practices, intervention services, care, and information with families, friends, schools, educational institutions, correctional systems, substance abuse programs, mental health programs, foster care systems, and other support organizations for tribal youth. Attention to the families and friends of tribal community members who recently died by suicide is encouraged as well. In addition, technical assistance will be provided to grantees through SAMHSA's Tribal Technical Assistance Center to support their ability to achieve their goals.

GLS Youth Suicide Prevention

The Garrett Lee Smith (GLS) Memorial Act authorizes SAMHSA to manage two significant youth suicide prevention programs and one resource center. The GLS State/Tribal Youth Suicide Prevention and Early Intervention grant program currently supports a total of 68 grantees which includes 29 tribes or tribal organizations in developing and implementing youth suicide prevention and early intervention strategies involving public-private collaborations among youth serving institutions. Recently announced tribal grantees include Native Americans for Community Action in Arizona, Confederated Salish and Kootenai Tribes in Montana, and the Yellowhawk Tribal Health Center in Oregon. The GLS Campus Suicide Prevention program currently provides funding to 82 institutions of higher education, inclusive of tribal colleges and universities. In a cross site evaluation of the GLS State/Tribal grant program, it was found that counties that had implemented grant supported youth suicide prevention activities had lower youth suicide rates than matched counties that had not implemented such activities in the year following those activities.

Project LAUNCH (Linking Actions for Unmet Needs in Children's Health)

Project LAUNCH is a grant program that invests in ensuring healthy physical, social, emotional, cognitive, and behavioral development of young children. This investment forms the foundation for later success in school and life and serves to protect against negative outcomes such as school dropout, drug and alcohol abuse, delinquency, and other physical, social, and emotional problems. Project LAUNCH grantees implement, monitor, and evaluate evidence-based prevention and promotion practices in partnership with a wide variety of community organizations and stakeholders. Project LAUNCH services are focused on five core strategies for promoting the social and emotional wellbeing of young children and their families: (1) increased developmental screening in a wide range of early childhood settings; (2) enhanced home visiting (with a focus on social/emotional wellbeing); (3) mental health consultation in early care and education settings; (4) integration of behavioral health into primary care; and (5) family strengthening/parent support. Each state/tribe and community's Project LAUNCH Council on Young Child Wellness monitors infrastructure development, implementation of evidence-based practices, and sustainability of successful practices through policy, planning, data, and funding decisions that improve services and outcomes for young children and their families.

Project LAUNCH has funded a total of 10 Tribal grantees. The Red Cliff Band of Lake Superior Chippewa completed a Project LAUNCH grant and tribal members have noted that the grant continues to serve as one of the powerful transformative mechanisms for the Red Cliff community. For example, during the grant period one leader noted that "I think the most important thing that LAUNCH is helping us do is looking at the difficult things the families have to juggle, making us take a step back and take a look from the family's point of view. And say, 'Okay, if I was in that position, what would I need to help me?' or better yet, asking the family, 'What do you need for help?'"

Children's Mental Health Initiative (CMHI)

The CMHI supports the development of comprehensive, community-based systems of care for children and youth with serious emotional disorders (SED) and their families. A system of care (SOC) is a strategic approach to the delivery of services and supports that incorporate family-driven, youth-guided, strength-based, and culturally and linguistically competent care in order to meet the physical, intellectual, emotional, cultural, and social needs of children and youth. These guiding principles also call for a broad array of effective services, individualized care, and coordination across child and youth-serving systems (e.g. juvenile justice, child welfare, education, primary care, and substance abuse) and have become standards for care throughout much of the nation. Recently announced CMHI grantees include Rocky Boy Health Board in Montana, the Santee Sioux Nation in North Dakota, and Lummi Nation in Washington.

National program evaluation data reported annually to Congress indicates that CMHI systems of care are successful, resulting in many favorable outcomes for children, youth, and their families, including:

- Sustained mental health disorder improvements for participating children and;
- Improvements in school attendance and achievement;
- Reductions in suicide-related behaviors;
- Decreases in the use of inpatient care and reduced costs due to fewer days in residential settings; and
- Significant reductions in contacts with law enforcement.

Circles of Care Grant Program

The Circles of Care program is the longest running SAMHSA grant program specifically designed for AI/AN communities. The program began in 1998 as a result of discussion and consultation with tribes and American Indian behavioral health professionals. To date, SAMHSA has awarded a total of $49 million in Circles of Care grants to 49 AI/AN communities. These communities have mobilized to develop the tools and resources necessary to build their own culturally competent systems of care model for children's mental health. Thus, many Circles of Care grantees go on to receive larger CMHI grants

In FY14, SAMHSA funded 11 tribes and tribal organization as part of a new cohort of Circles of Care grantees. Among the grantees include the Osage Tribe of Indians in Oklahoma, the Makah Tribe in Washington, and the Red Cliff Band of Lake Superior Chippewa in Wisconsin.

Conclusion

Thank you again for this opportunity to discuss children's mental health as it relates to preventing and addressing childhood trauma in Indian Country. I hope you can see that this issue is a major priority for SAMHSA and recent activities such as the establishment of our OTAP, release of the trauma concept paper, and hosting this week's Native Youth Conference underscore our dedication. I would now be pleased to answer any questions that you may have.

The CHAIRMAN. Kana, thank you for your testimony.

Rick?

STATEMENT OF RICK VAN DEN POL, PH.D., DIRECTOR AND PRINCIPAL INVESTIGATOR, INSTITUTE OF EDUCATIONAL RESEARCH AND SERVICE, THE UNIVERSITY OF MONTANA NATIONAL NATIVE CHILDREN'S TRAUMA CENTER

Dr. VAN DEN POL. Thank you for the invitation.

My name is Rick van den Pol. I serve as Principal Investigator at the National Native Children's Trauma Center at the University of Montana.

I have been a professor at the University of Montana tenured in psychology and education for 33 years. I have worked with children who have trauma for 33 years but only about half the time did I know what trauma was.

Only about half the time was I able to provide trauma-informed, effective services. This is a very young field and the science is very young. I cannot give you an authentic perspective or an authentic Native perspective on childhood trauma but as principal investigator, I can share with you some findings from our work in the National Native Children's Trauma Center.

In my written testimony, I have five exhibits. The first is a chapter written for pediatricians about the impact of trauma on the developing child and the developing brain. A very important component of that message is missing from the national dialogue about ACE's, Adverse Childhood Experiences.

The missing component is the treatability of childhood trauma. We absolutely want to invest in long term prevention. I am reminded of a statement sometimes attributed to Chief Joseph that we need to consider the impacts of our actions on the next seven generations. But, the present Congress needs to have some solutions it can implement more quickly than that.

The second exhibit is a handout from the National Child Traumatic Stress Network, the network created by the National Child Traumatic Stress Initiative of SAMHSA.

The handout speaks to the treatability of trauma, the newness of the science and the importance of training clinicians who are currently practicing on an in-service basis and new clinicians as they come through our graduate and medical schools.

The third finding I share with you is research performed by Dr. Mary Kaas and colleagues, not associated with our center. They believe that the prevalence of childhood trauma in Indian Country is probably about twice as bad as the statistic you cited, Mr. Chairman.

According to them, using the ACE 4 point scale, about five times as many individuals in their sample of Native Americans tested at 4 ACE points. In the original fluidity sample published by the Centers for Disease Control, it was 20 percent of that rate and there were also symptoms of trauma present.

The fourth exhibit I offered is work done by one of my colleagues, Dr. Aaron Morsette, who was then a graduate student working at our center. Aaron tested a trauma treatment in three different reservation schools in the northern plains and found very positive results.

Native students, who qualified, who presented with trauma, on average, two-thirds showed significant reductions after ten hours of participation with a group of peers and more than half showed measurable reductions in symptoms of depression.

Dr. Morsette, as we all were, has been puzzled by the prevalence of trauma in Indian people. His dissertation, yet unpublished but cited and discoverable on the Internet, examined the etiology of trauma in one reservation school population, using a very creative but valid statistic.

Dr. Morsette was able to identify that it was grief and loss that appeared to contribute more powerfully mathematically to trauma symptoms than violence exposure. This is quite revolutionary as we always screen for violence exposure but screening for traumatic grief is not part of our standard practice yet.

I asked Dr. Morsette, at his dissertation defense, why he did that and he said, it just didn't ring true for me and it didn't seem to be true for my friends and our people, so I had to put some science to it.

I would share three recommendations, not the official position of the University of Montana but my own on what we can do immediately.

Immediately, we need to make sure that we continue to train doctoral level MDs and PhDs, clinicians and researchers who are themselves Native. We cannot achieve our goals of self determination if in the next generation, it is non-Natives trying to lead the discussion about policy, research and practice.

Second, the National Child and Traumatic Stress Initiative supports 80 funded centers with a budget of about $50 million. With a budget of about $75 million, that number could increase to about 120. That network has been extraordinarily effective across the Nation and extraordinarily effective in addressing the needs of Native children with trauma.

Finally, I would like to endorse the comment of Director Enomoto.

Thank you for allowing us to infuse traditional cultural healing with evidence-based scientific approaches to trauma treatment. I think that is why we have been able to demonstrate the results that we have.

I actually never thought I would sit in a setting such as this and hear a Federal official say that was not only permissible but encouraged. We really have come a long way.

Thank you.

[The prepared statement of Dr. van den Pol follows:]

PREPARED STATEMENT OF RICK VAN DEN POL, PH.D., DIRECTOR AND PRINCIPAL
INVESTIGATOR, INSTITUTE OF EDUCATIONAL RESEARCH AND SERVICE,   THE
UNIVERSITY OF MONTANA NATIONAL NATIVE CHILDREN'S TRAUMA CENTER

Biography: Rick VandenPol has been a Professor at the University of Montana for 33 years, tenured in the departments of Psychology and Education. For the past 14 years he has served as Principal Investigator of the National Native Children's Trauma Center. That Center, a member of the National Child Traumatic Stress Network, is the only federally-funded (SAMHSA/NCTSI) Childhood Trauma Treatment and Adaptation Center charged with disseminating information on childhood trauma in Indian Country throughout the United States.

Disclaimer: Faculty members of the University of Montana are obligated to make public their professional conclusion and to explicitly note that such conclusions of individual conclusions and do not necessarily reflect the official policy of the University of Montana, the MUS Board of Regents, or any federal agency who supports sponsored research and service grant activities.

Finding 1 Child traumatic stress is similar to adult post traumatic stress disorder as seen in combat veterans. However, it manifests differently due to human development. Early exposure to adverse childhood experiences (victim of violence, witness to violence, loss of loved one) is associated with negative public health outcomes including elevated morbidity, mortality, suicide, chemical dependence, marital dissatisfaction, and unemployment).

Finding 1.1 Adverse childhood experiences are associated with visible changes in brain anatomy.

Finding 1.2 Adverse childhood experiences are treatable, and early effects of adversity can be mitigated or eliminated with effective evidence-based treatment.

Source: Exhibit 1

Citation: VandenPol, R. and Manning, R. (2015). Child Abuse and the Emergence of the Diagnosis of Developmental Trauma. In J. Jones (Ed.)(*Physician's Guide to Mental Health Disorders in Childhood Maltreatment.*) St. Louis, MO: STM Learning

Finding 2 Adverse childhood exposure and symptoms of child traumatic stress can be treated effectively and economically. The national resource for such treatment is the National Child Traumatic Stress Network.

Source: Exhibit II. Description of National Child Traumatic Stress Network (handout).

Finding 3 The prevalence of adverse childhood experience and symptoms of trauma appear to be more than 500% higher among some American Indian Tribes.

Source: Exhibit III

Citation: Mary P. Koss, PhD, Nicole P. Yuan, PhD, Douglas Dightman, MPH, Ronald J. Prince, MS, Mona Polacca, MSW, Byron Sanderson, MSW(late), David Goldman, MD. (2003). Adverse Childhood Exposures and Alcohol Dependence Among Seven Native American Tribes. *American Journal of Preventive Medicine*, 25(3), 238–244.

Finding 4 Native youth with symptoms of childhood traumatic stress can be treated effective by economical interventions delivered in middle schools.

Source: Exhibit IV

Citation: Morsette, A., van den Pol, R., Schuldberg, D. , Swaney, G.. & Stolle, D. (2012). Cognitive behavioral treatment for trauma symptoms in American Indian youth: Preliminary findings and issues in evidence-based practice and reservation culture. *Advances in School Mental Health Promotion*, 5,1. 51 – 62.

Finding 5 While Native Americans may have higher levels of trauma than other Americans, emerging research suggests that trauma symptoms are more strongly related to loss and bereavement than to violence exposure.

Source: Exhibit V

Citation: Morsette, A. Examining the role of grief in the etiology of Posttraumatic Stress Disorder (PTSD) symptoms in American Indian adolescents (unpublished doctoral dissertation), posted http://search.proquest.com.weblib.lib.umt.edu:8080/pqdtft/docview/304943105/16CB1B1678EA49A0P Q/2?accountid=14593

*The exhibits referred to have been retained in the Committee files.

The CHAIRMAN. Thank you, Rick.
Verné.

STATEMENT OF VERNE BOERNER, PRESIDENT/CEO, ALASKA NATIVE HEALTH BOARD

Ms. BOERNER. Chairman Tester, Vice Chairman Barrasso, and members of the Committee, my name is Verné Boerner. I am the President and CEO of the Alaska Native Health Board.

I submit this statement for the record. I would also like to note that ANHB's testimony is supported by the National Indian Health Board.

Thank you for inviting me to provide input on protecting our children. We all share in this awesome obligation. No group this size is more vulnerable, more dependent, or whose experiences will determine the health and prosperity of our people.

I sit here before you with two asks that go toward breaking the cycle of violence and abuse. Repeal Section 910 of the Violence Against Women Act. We will be watching for the Safe Families and Villages Act and how that progresses as well.

The second ask is to increase the Indian Health Service behavioral health funds in a non-grant and non-competitive manner and confer other Federal resources such as the Prevention and Health Fund to the IHS.

I am extremely appreciative of my co-panelists who have painted a picture and have defined so well the impacts of childhood trauma. I offer to you a face to go with those numbers.

I was sexually abused from the time I was nine years old until 14. I lived in fear and silence those years. When the man who abused me told me that my sister, who turned nine years old, was ready, I went to the police.

During those years, our family experienced other abuses as well. The aftermath was also quite devastating. I have to lift my mother up for her strength and support during that time. However, my sister went through this during her formative years. She later became an alcoholic. She too got involved with abusive men and turned away from the good man in her life.

She died three days before her 29th birthday, not from overdose or poisoning but because she was trying to quit.

A most painful fact is that my story is not unique. It is far too common. In Alaska, over 50 percent of Alaska Native women report having experienced some form of abuse. It is from these experiences and the women and children in our communities that I express my gratitude to my Senators, Lisa Murkowski and Mark Begich, for your work and efforts to repeal Section 910 of the Violence Against Women Act. Thank you.

Addressing violence against women is a key component of breaking the cycle and preventing the associated childhood trauma.

Regarding my second ask, the U.S. Government engages with tribes on a government-to-government basis seeking input on the Indian Health Service budget formulation process. Tribes in Alaska and nationally have consistently identified behavioral health as a key funding priority.

The increase should not come at the expense of other IHS services and programs. Its system is already stressed and plagued by chronic under funding. I do understand the fiscal constraints that we face as a Nation, but the cost of not breaking the cycle of violence and abuse is higher still.

Furthermore, tribes have proven to be a good investment and have demonstrated innovation and capacity in designing and/or participating in effective projects. I would like to highlight the efforts of two of ANHB's members.

The Alaska Native Tribal Health Consortium has long engaged in scientifically rigorous, culturally informed or modified approaches, one of which is the Alaska Native Adverse Childhood Experiences Study.

This study is contributing to the general body of knowledge regarding the unique conditions and impacts that adverse childhood experiences have in the varied settings throughout our State.

The second is, the Southcentral Foundation has created the Family Wellness Warriors Initiative. There are many things I can say about this program and its integration with others, but due to the lack of time, I will focus on one special aspect.

It incorporates the men. It seeks to celebrate their traditional role as protectors and engages them as heroes and champions.

These are just two of the many approaches out there. They are doing meaningful work. Please support the efforts and allocate more resources so that together we can eliminate two of the most infrequent levels of childhood trauma.

Thank you.

[The prepared statement of Ms. Boerner follows:]

PREPARED STATEMENT OF VERNÉ BOERNER, PRESIDENT/CEO, ALASKA NATIVE
HEALTH BOARD

Chairman Tester, Vice Chairman Barrasso and Members of the Committee:

Thank you for the opportunity to provide input for this hearing addressing one of our greatest charges, our children. My name is Verné Boerner. I am the President and CEO of the Alaska Native Health Board (ANHB) and a member of the Indian Health Service Budget Formulation Workgroup. Established in 1968, ANHB serves as Alaska's statewide voice on Alaska Native health issues. Our 26 member organizations deliver health care programs and services to over 143,000 Alaska Native and American Indian people residing in the state of Alaska. ANHB's mission is to promote the spiritual, physical, mental, social, and cultural wellbeing and pride of Alaska Native people.

By way of introduction, my appreciation for your having this hearing is personal as I was sexually abused from the time I was 9 years old until I was 14. I lived in silence and fear for all that time until right before I went to the police. What prompted me to go to the police was when my sister turned 9 years old the abuser told me she was ''ready.''

In addition, my mother and older brother were victims of domestic violence, we spent nights at women's shelters, and my younger sister started to experience the abuse I had and aftermath of the full breakdown of the family unit. She later became an alcoholic and involved in abusive relationships. She passed away three days before her 29th birthday from ''complications due to chronic ethanolism.'' Her death was categorized as ''Natural.'' I know it is a technical term, but there is nothing natural about that.

Requests. With regard to preventing and addressing childhood trauma in Indian Country, ANHB has two asks:

1. Repeal Section 910 (the Alaska exception) of the Violence Against Women Act (VAWA), and

2. Increase Indian Health Service behavioral health program funds in a non-grant and non-competitive manner and provide other federal sources such as the Prevention and Public Health Fund.

As of the time of this writing, we did not have a copy of the recommendations of November 18 to the Attorney General regarding trauma among Native children, but we look forward to reviewing the report and making further comments.

Repeal of Section 910 of the Violence Against Women Act

We support repeal of the ''Alaska exception'' to the Violence Against Women Act. While we recognize the unique situation in Alaska, it is clear that the current system is failing our women and families. The Tribal governments in Alaska are not able to carry out local, culturally relevant solutions to effectively address the lack of law enforcement and prosecution in villages that allows perpetrators to slip through the cracks. The law enforcement and judicial systems created and administered by Indian tribes or tribal organizations within Alaska will be more responsive to the need for greater local control and accountability in the administration of justice than centralized State of Alaska systems. (Kastelic, 2014)

We specifically extend our appreciation to Senator Murkowski and Senator Begich for their support and efforts to repeal the Alaska exception of the Violence Against Women Act. Thank you also, Senator Murkowski, for your emphasis on finding increased resources for courts in Alaska to deal with what would be expanded VAWA authority.

Alaska Native women face domestic and sexual violence in the home at disproportionate rates and in many cases this violence is witnessed and/or experienced by children in the home, as was the case in my family. And sadly, I personally witnessed the long-term effects of trauma with my sister. According to the National Indian Child Welfare Association, Alaska Native children made up 17.3 percent of

Alaska's child population, yet they represented 50.1 percent of the substantiated reports of maltreatment. (Kastelic, 2014). No matter the challenges, we must endeavor to develop the jurisdictional framework in Alaska to enable tribal communities to protect our families.

Addressing violence against women is a key component of breaking the cycle and preventing the associated childhood trauma.

Increase Funding for Behavioral Health

Indian Health Service

The IHS Budget Formulation Process is a government-to-government consultation process and is reflective of the tribes' own determined priorities. Behavioral health and Alcohol and Substance Abuse Programs have consistently been identified as priorities. Funding to these IHS programs, granted in a non-competitive and non-grant manner, offers the greatest flexibilities to tribes to exercise self-determination, and has a track record of success. ANHB urges Congress to enact the Budget Formulation Workgroup's recommendation that Mental Health funding be increased by $51.5 million above the President's FY 2015 request for a total of $134 million.

Tribes think holistically and they have specified that a continuum of care for both prevention and treatment through integrated behavioral health programs is needed. Congress agreed, codifying it in the Indian Health Care Improvement Act (IHCIA). Unfortunately to date, the new authorities in the IHCIA have not had the appropriations needed to implement the provisions.

While we can point to the IHS budget increasing in recent years, those increases are in particular areas—most welcome, to be sure—but the area of behavioral health has not seen program increases.

Prevention and Public Health Fund

It was encouraging when the Administration proposed as part of the FY 2012 budget to allocate $50 million of the Affordable Care Act (ACA) Prevention and Public Health Fund (PPH) for coordinated tribal services to prevent substance abuse and suicide. The Administration proposed to administer the program through SAMHSA, with funding being provided to each applicant tribe and additional funding based on population and need. While the PPH funding does not need to be appropriated ($17.7 billion over ten years, some of which has been rescinded) because it is mandatory funding. Congress must allocate from the Fund on an annual basis, and unfortunately did not allocate the funds for tribes as requested by the Administration.

We find that funding provided directly to tribal organizations works better than having it filter through the state or another organization and allows us to better design services, including the inclusion of culturally appropriate services. We ask Congress to allocate $50 million of the PPH Fund to the Indian Health Service for behavioral health services and that it be on a recurring basis.

Alaska Approaches

Tribal programs in Alaska have taken a variety of approaches toward preventing and addressing childhood trauma. These approaches are innovative, scientifically rigorous, and are community and culturally based. The following are just a few of the activities that Alaska tribes have implemented.

Alaska Native Tribal Health Consortium

The Alaska Native Tribal Health Consortium's vision is that Alaska Native people are the healthiest in the world. To achieve this vision, Alaska Native people need healthy families and healthy communities. Domestic violence and sexual violence (DV/SV) can profoundly wound individuals, families and whole communities. It is common to hear that DV/SV disproportionately affects Alaska Native people. By ensuring we have reliable data and by monitoring changes over time, we can better understand which programs and interventions are most successful. The ANTHC Adverse Childhood Experiences Study adds to the growing literature and general understanding of the problem. Every child, teen, pregnant woman, adult, and Elder is precious and deserves to live a life without violence. Having communities without DV and SV would contribute to making the vision of Alaska Native people as the healthiest people in the world a reality. (Alaska Native Tribal Health Consortium, 2013)

Yukon Kuskokwim Health Corporation

Yukon Kuskokwim Health Corporation's (YKHC) incorporated trauma-informed services by implementing the Adverse Childhood Experiences (ACEs) questionnaire, including translating the questionnaire into Yupik. YKHC's staff is comprised of all Native Alaskans who have personal experience with trauma. The questionnaire has been given to each of their clients entering the Crisis Respite Center, and has also been administered to the general population at several Family Wellness/Suicide Prevention gatherings in the YKHC area of Alaska. The biggest reaction from YKHC's clients has been, ''I've never told anyone this before.'' Many are relieved that someone is asking them about trauma and is willing to help. YKHC found that the most valuable use of the ACEs Survey was to open a conversation with the client and begin to work through their residual responses to trauma. (Bryan)

Tanana Chiefs Conference

Tanana Chiefs Conference (TCC) also uses a Trauma-informed Services approach, which begins when a new client is screened into the various programs TCC offers. TCC's approach empowers clients as they are given choices as to how long, and what kind of therapy they will accept, and what issues to address. TCC offers early intervention and prevention therapies as well as longer styles of therapy. This approach builds on each client's individual strengths and cultural ties, which are seen as major components to the program. The therapist and clients work together as equals in developing a treatment plan; if it is determined that one is needed. The goal is to increase the client's skills to allow them to manage their symptoms and reactions on their own.'' (Bryan)

Southcentral Foundation

For more than 15 years, Alaska Native people have been leading the charge to end domestic violence, child abuse and child neglect in Alaska through Southcentral Foundation's (SCF) Family Wellness Warriors Initiative (FWWI). SCF's strategies are based on Alaska Native cultural strengths and bringing back traditional values that are protective of family wellness. FWWI helps build the capacity of individuals, families and communities to reverse the trends of domestic violence and child maltreatment. Over a period of many years, we have been successful in providing the education, tools and skills needed to bring awareness to the issues; creating safe environments for sharing and healing; and initiating changes in attitudes, behaviors, and beliefs.

The work of ending domestic violence, child abuse and child neglect is too important to keep it within the bounds of a few programs or services. For broader impact, FWWI is also built into the structure and design of SCF's Nuka System of Care. Every year, new improvements are made to the way that trauma and abuse are assessed and responded to throughout the health care system. (Southcentral Foundation, 2014)

In closing, Alaska Native Health Board thanks you for your attention to child trauma issues. We believe that repealing Section 910 of the Violence Against Women Act and increased resources for tribal behavioral health services will substantially help break the cycle of childhood trauma in tribal communities.

***

Works Cited

Alaska Native Tribal Health Consortium. (2013, March). Retrieved November 16, 2014, from ANTHC Today: *http://www.anthctoday.org/epicenter/publications/alaskanativefamilies/dvsaBulletin\2ndled\final.pdf*

Bryan, M. (n.d.). ATTC Network. Retrieved November 16, 2014, from *http://www.attcnetwork.org/find/news/attcnews/epubs/addmsg/documents/Trauma\Part\3%20May%2031.pdf*

Kastelic, S. (2014). *Deputy Director, National Indian Child Welfare Association.* Portland: National Indian Child Welfare Association.

Southcentral Foundation. (2014, January). Southcentral Foundation. Retrieved November 16, 2014, from Southcentral Foundation: *https://www.southcentralfoundation.com/newsletter/2014JanFebANN.pdf*

The CHAIRMAN. Thank you all for your testimony. It is very much appreciated.

We will do five minute rounds. I will start with you, Mr. Listenbee.

Communities often seek to integrate traditional healing practice into programs aimed at addressing trauma. Can you tell me what obstacles exist to allow for traditional healing programs to happen?

Mr. LISTENBEE. Senator, we know from the report submitted by the advisory committee yesterday that incorporating traditional healing programs into current practices and therapeutic practices is really important.

We know that one-third of children who have been given an opportunity to use traditional healing methods or traditional cultural healing, persons have chosen that over other approaches. We know that half of the adults have chosen those approaches over other approaches as well.

We think it is very important. We encourage it and we have tried to implement that in the various programs that we have developed throughout the Department of Justice.

The CHAIRMAN. You don't see any roadblocks though?

Mr. LISTENBEE. Senator, as we know from the report that was submitted yesterday, there are a number of problems and issues involved with developing new approaches and incorporating traditional approaches into current practices.

We know these are things that have to be carefully considered and reviewed. As we go forward in terms of implementing the recommendations of the report, we expect that we will be working closely with experts in the field to help develop more effective approaches.

The CHAIRMAN. I would just say that if there are roadblocks, we need to find out how we can resolve those roadblocks because I think this could add to the effectiveness of any sort of programs out there.

Dr. van den Pol, I have a question for you.

Your testimony mentions that new research suggests that trauma may be tied more to loss and bereavement than to violence. Can you tell me what that means for Indian Country?

Dr. VAN DEN POL. Mr. Chairman, my impression is subjective and has not been subjected to any kind of systematic study but in my conversations with many Native colleagues, there is a vast disparity in the number of deaths of loved ones they have experienced as opposed to my non-Native colleagues.

This is something that comes up as a surprising matter anecdotally and I don't know of anyone who has looked at it in a systematic fashion. When Dr. Morsette was working with clients in his trauma treatment regimen, he did not ask them, what is wrong with you? He asked them, what happened to you?

What they talked about was having their grandma die from cancer or losing a sibling to an accident. It seems that qualitative research is very suggestive about child traumatic grief, particularly for Native youth.

The CHAIRMAN. I am going to turn the Chair over to Senator Cantwell.

Senator CANTWELL. [Presiding] Thank you.

Senator Murkowski?

Senator MURKOWSKI. Thank you, Madam Chair.

I will be brief. Hopefully the rest of my colleagues can move forward.

I want to thank all of you, particularly Verné, for your testimony. It was truly spoken from the heart.

Know that I am committed. We are going to get this Section 910 repealed, get that done and over with.

I also want to acknowledge Valerie Davidson in the room who has been on the Task Force on American Indians and Alaska Native Children Exposed to Violence. I really appreciate your work on that, Val. Thank you for that.

There has been a lot of discussion about the funding and how do we make this available through grants. You have mentioned non-grant, IHS funds. This is going to be a query to you, Administrator Listenbee.

When we talk about grants, we appreciate the variability of that funding. The fact of the matter is that not only do our tribal justice programs have to be adequately funded but they need to occur on an annual basis. You need to be able to rely on them.

Right now, our tribes in Alaska do not receive Department of Interior law enforcement nor tribal court funds. I am working on that. I am on the Interior Appropriations Committee. I think we are going to be in a position to perhaps advance that.

I am wondering whether the Department of Justice would be willing to put forward a formula-funded structure for tribal justice programs? We have to be able to have the resources to provide for this level of safety and security.

Can you at least tell us that you are going to look at it? We have to make some headway on this.

Mr. LISTENBEE. Senator, what we know is that we agree with the advisory committee that the current method for providing funding for unique financial and criminal justice issues in Alaska does not really address the concerns. We recognized this issue some time ago because the tribes brought it to our attention.

At the Justice Department, we developed the Coordinated Tribal Assistance Solicitation Process in 2010 and we have been using that since then. This process allows the Department to streamline the application process and to more effectively address specific concerns raised by the tribes.

It also gives American Indian and Alaska Native communities the opportunity to focus their concerns on their most important criminal justice and public safety issues and then to develop innovative programs and evidence-based practices to address them.

Along with that, Senator, since fiscal year 2011, the President's Office of Justice Programs Submission of Budget has indicated and requested a 7 percent setaside that would be used for this particular purpose.

We are hoping that 7 percent setaside will be coming forth sometime in the not too distant future.

Senator MURKOWSKI. I would really encourage that. Quite honestly, folks don't want to hear that we are engaged in more process. They want to know that we have resources on the ground. They know that tribal courts are funded in the lower 48; they know that they are not funded in Alaska. That doesn't make sense to them; it doesn't make sense to me.

We are going to be working on this. We would like the Department of Justice to be working with us.

Very quickly, Dr. Roubideaux, we have had this conversation before about our village-built clinic program and the fact that these clinics do not have the funding. They simply do not have the funding and yet when we want to make sure that we have behavioral health aides, when we want to make sure that we have our community health aides who can be that resource for those who have been violated, for those who do need that help, we don't have these systems in place.

I was just in a conversation yesterday where once again, we are concerned that we are not getting any support from the Administration on ensuring that our village health clinics are adequately funded.

We have to have these instruments in place. We have to have the protective side through the ability to enforce some level of justice, but we also have to have the health side. You have got to help us with these village-built clinics. You have got to help us. Yes?

Dr. ROUBIDEAUX. Well, yes, we do want to help. That is why we have been working——

Senator MURKOWSKI. But we have not seen that through the budgets put forth by this Administration. We have seen zero help there. We need you to help us. I am going to be very direct with that because we are going to demand that you help us.

We have been very polite and we have waited a long time. In the meantime, we are losing what we have built.

Dr. ROUBIDEAUX. I have heard loud and clear from the tribes. It is a very important issue for Alaska and I would like to work with you on that.

Senator MURKOWSKI. It is very important. Thank you.

Senator CANTWELL. Senator Heitkamp.

Senator HEITKAMP. I have just a couple quick comments. Thank you all for your work in this very important area and thank you for your personal testimony. It is so important that we tell the stories and the truth about what really is going on.

I have a question. None of you mentioned as a potential solution better screening of children when they enter the education system. I am wondering if anyone wants to comment on whether that is a strategy we are pursuing anywhere and if we have better diagnosis which gives us a better opportunity for early intervention and better treatment options and outcomes?

Ms. BOERNER. Yes, I do know that the Tanana Chiefs Conference in Alaska has implemented such a program. I can ask them to provide more information. I will definitely make sure we get that to you. I do know they are looking at early intervention and early screening starting with the school age kids.

Yes, there are programs out there. I will get more information for you.

Ms. ENOMOTO. We are also working on developing clinical measures as well as epidemiological measures to measure trauma in primary care settings and other settings where we have children and adults, as well as in our surveillance instruments looking at measuring trauma nationwide as it relates to mental health and substance abuse.

Senator HEITKAMP. One of the kind of pushes for this Committee hearing came out of some work that I was doing in North Dakota with a woman there who is dealing with treatment of historic trauma.

Great results are being experienced. When we deal with it on the front end, we know we have a higher graduation rate, more secure communities, more secure kids and so this is something we can't let another generation go and say, we know you feel our pain, we just want you to do something about it.

This idea that we are working on it in the face of these statistics is not an adequate response. I think you all know that.

I will close with that.

Senator CANTWELL. Thank you, Senator Heitkamp.

Thank you for your leadership. You have been quite vocal on the importance of this to Indian Country health overall. We appreciate it.

I would like to go back to you Mr. Listenbee, about the CTAS grants, the coordinated tribal assistance solicitation the Department of Justice does.

I was quoting your statistics about 75 percent of deaths of American Indian and Alaska Native youth from the ages of 12–20, that about 75 percent of that is related to assaults, homicide or suicide. The coordinated tribal assistance solicitation I am assuming are trying to tackle or get at that issue.

I know in the case of the Tulalips, they had one last year for over $1 million. I am asking about the metrics that the department uses to measure the results of those grants. What are the kinds of activities they are undertaking to try to lower that statistic of 75 percent?

Mr. LISTENBEE. Senator, first of all, that statistic is actually supported and comes from research done by Dolores Subia Bigfoot, a member of the advisory committee, based upon studies that she performed. It is a very solid fact.

In terms of what the department is doing, through the CTAS programs, we have a wide range of efforts that are available to address this specific issue. Tribes are permitted, in the various purpose areas, to follow through and address this particular issue.

One of the specific things we are doing through the Office of Juvenile Justice and Delinquency Prevention is tribal healing and wellness courts. We introduced that in fiscal year 2014. There are five courts that have been selected.

Our purpose is to use traditional approaches and culturally specific approaches combined with basic tenets of drug courts to help children who have been exposed to alcohol abuse. We are hoping that will be helpful. It goes up to age 21.

Senator CANTWELL. What are some of the measurements you are using on those grants? How are you coming back and saying, here is the amount of money we have spent and how are we being successful with this? What measurements are you using?

Mr. LISTENBEE. Throughout the Department of Justice and Office of Justice Programs, we have some very standard metrics that we use to measure the effectiveness of all of our grants. We are applying the same metrics to the specific tribal grants we have also.

Senator CANTWELL. If you don't have those today, could you get them to me or if you have some idea about what they are, either way?

Mr. LISTENBEE. We are willing to provide that information to you.

Senator CANTWELL. Okay, but those are being measured you are saying?

Mr. LISTENBEE. Yes.

Senator CANTWELL. Have you come up with anything you would like to change based on those metrics?

Mr. LISTENBEE. At this point in time, Senator, I will have to get back to you on that. I don't have any metrics information with me that would allow me to provide you with specific information about that.

Senator CANTWELL. Okay.

Dr. Roubideaux, I wanted to ask you about better coordination between mental health and other tribal services. In my State, we are embarking on trying to integrate both behavioral health and primary care services for the Medicaid population.

What is happening in Indian Country to try to integrate those same services?

Dr. ROUBIDEAUX. I am glad to hear that because we are very committed to integrating behavioral health into primary care. We have our Improving Patient Care Program which is our patient centered medical home initiative now in 172 sites.

Next month, their training session is going to be on integration of behavioral health into primary care, making sure that we can do that so that we can identify and treat these conditions earlier.

Senator CANTWELL. What do you think that means? What types of services? I have been impressed as I have traveled around various Indian Country health care facilities. For example, in Anchorage, the facility there is almost like the community hub. Everybody hangs out there. That is a very positive environment where you can see issues of concern or frustration on the behavioral side may be brought up right in the environment.

I have been to other places where the health care delivery system is at one end of the community and maybe not even that frequently used unless someone absolutely needs it.

How are we getting to integration of behavioral health?

Dr. ROUBIDEAUX. With our Improving Patient Care Program, it helps coordinate the team of providers rather than having mental health over here, primary care there, dental here and pharmacy there. The whole team of providers is working together to help have a better coordinated response to helping identify, diagnose and treat the patients.

It is something that we see as helping. Patients are telling us that they are more satisfied and that it creates a more welcoming environment as you described. I think we share the same vision of that is where we want our system to go.

Through the training we are providing, the structure, through the accreditation process for patient center medical homes, we are really hoping that will help us move towards that goal.

Senator CANTWELL. What about programs specifically on the reservations? What ideas do you have, any of the panelists, for creating better awareness on tribal reservations and an entry point for discussion, even if it is just education and training for tribal leaders or tribal elders or ways to identify problems?

Dr. ROUBIDEAUX. For the Indian Health Service, we do a lot of training in partnership with tribes on mental health, alcohol and substance abuse, child maltreatment and all those issues. They give us opportunities to share best practices.

In a number of our programs, we have a lot of evidence-based and practice-based programs that can be replicated in other areas. That includes not only doing the clinical component of it, but also incorporating tradition and culture because we really think that is the way we are going to be able to address these problems more effectively.

We have been using more webinars, tele-behavioral health and more training to try to make sure that we are not just training our staff, but community members, tribal leaders and youth. We are working with the schools as well.

Senator CANTWELL. These statistics are so shocking. As my colleague from Alaska said, she has been to places and I have certainly been to places where the youth have expressed their own frustrations.

My question is, what can we do to better orient these programs to somebody really being on site or integration, in this case, with the school systems so that these kinds of concerns, anxieties or pressure points by students from the behavioral health side can be more directly answered immediately, brought to the surface, developed or even things their friends and classmates can say, these are some of the things that are going on here, this is what needs to be dealt with.

I see you nodding, Dr. van den Pol. Do you have something to add to that?

Dr. VAN DEN POL. I am not sure that I do. I was agreeing enthusiastically with your remarks.

I think there is huge potential in schools to address trauma. One of the early studies of trauma treatment was after Hurricane Katrina, we were invited to Jefferson Parish to work in the school there.

One of our counterparts who developed the Cognitive Behavioral Intervention for Trauma in Schools, Dr. Lisa Jaycox with the RAND Corporation, evaluated a group of students who had been through Katrina and were sent to a clinic for mental health treatment and students who were seen in school who received the same treatment.

I believe the students in the school were three to four times more likely to engage with the treatment program than students going to the clinic.

We know where the kids are and we can get them there. Sometimes we need consent for certain kinds of treatments but I think in terms of looking for efficient and effective return on investments, one setting where we are going to find kids who have trauma is in schools.

Senator CANTWELL. Thank you.

Ms. Boerner, did you want to add something to that?

Ms. BOERNER. I do. Within the Indian Health Care Improvement Act there are unfunded authorities that have been passed, one of which creates a continuum of care within behavioral health issues.

One of the recommendations that came from Alaska tribes was to embark on training and education programs to encourage more tribal members to enter the field. That is something where perhaps existing practitioners may be able to develop a program where they are more present and more a part.

Hopefully we reduce some of the stigmatization that exists out there so there can be more open, less taboo discussions, perhaps creating that interest within our youth to enter the field.

Senator CANTWELL. I am sorry, I had to confer with my colleagues. The Chairman might be returning.

You are saying you think there are certain subjects that right now there is a problem because people don't want them more openly discussed and we should be discussing them more openly?

Ms. BOERNER. I believe that we might be able to pique the interest of our youth if we are more present out there with these programs and create more of a mentorship, an involvement.

I think there is a lot of stigmatization and a lot of fear around mental health and behavioral health issues that is a barrier. It is not something I think many of our youth are even considering as a possible future.

I think if you get more of the practitioners out there and involved in a sort of mentoring program, thinking of the long term effects of having more practitioners and the seventh generation concept.

What we do today has those lasting impacts. Today, if our action is if we need something in the immediate, that is something that perhaps we can do, create a greater visibility of how beneficial this field can be to our people, then perhaps we will get those kids involved.

Then down the line our grandchildren's grandchildren will be more involved and a part of the conceptualization and creation of those programs.

Senator CANTWELL. Not to put you on the spot about it, but how do you think that is best achieved? How do you think destigmatizing behavioral health could be accomplished?

Ms. BOERNER. One reason why I am open about my own personal experiences is because it is something that is filled with taboo and the discussions are not necessarily happening. I am in a place personally where I feel I can be open and I can share those things.

I have certain protective factors I think that allow me to do that and I certainly understand others do not have that but having and opening that conversation starts to release a lot. Once people start opening up and some of what I have read from the Yukon Kuskokwim when they have implemented the ACE study, some of the members said, I have never shown that before. It is sort of like an ''aha'' moment.

I think having them out there, having them visible just creates a natural situation where the conversations are happening. Once that happens, it starts breaking down those barriers and builds the understanding.

Senator CANTWELL. Thank you for sharing that and for what you are trying to do to break down the barriers.

Ms. Enomoto, did you have a comment?

Ms. ENOMOTO. At SAMHSA, since the time of Columbine and the unfortunate events there, SAMHSA has had a long track record of partnering with the Department of Education and the Department of Justice in addressing school violence and working to promote mental health in schools and prevent violence in schools.

Under the President's Now Is the Time Initiative, we have started to take that to scale where we want to launch a nationwide effort to integrate schools, communities and behavioral health to really promote both mental health literacy, violence prevention and create positive school climates in every school in America.

At SAMHSA, we would look forward to partnering with BIE, with tribes and their tribal schools to expand models such as Safe Schools, Healthy Students and mental health first aid for youth in Indian Country.

Senator CANTWELL. What do you think the next step is? Is it an actual agreement with BIE? We clearly see from the statistics we have a great need. We may be seeing there are some cultural issues or something that may be blocking us.

Obviously moving to more outreach efforts directly in the community, you can see they are desperately needed.

Ms. ENOMOTO. Right. We have begun conversations with BIA. We would welcome more opportunities to partner with them on that.

Senator CANTWELL. Okay.

Dr. Roubideaux, I would like to ask you about the bed shortage issue. Obviously, we cannot simply board people at the county jail. Our State is moving towards trying to deal with this. How do we deal with the shortage of psychiatric beds in Indian Country?

Dr. ROUBIDEAUX. It is a significant problem you have raised. It is something we definitely need to work more on. It is an issue, for example, with youth we have our youth regional treatment centers in 12 areas but they have a certain number of beds.

In terms of how we pay for those, we have our Purchase and Referred Care Program where we pay for the services. As the funding has been increased over the past few years, thank you for your advocacy on that, we are able to pay for more referrals and that would help us pay for more of those services if beds are available. Bed availability is a huge issue.

Senator CANTWELL. Do you have an estimate of what it would actually take to service Indian Country? Do you have a number of how many psychiatric beds you actually think we need and what the distribution looks like?

Dr. ROUBIDEAUX. I would be happy to talk with my staff and get back to you with an estimate.

Senator CANTWELL. Thank you.

Let me see if I had any other questions for anyone else on the panel.

Mr. Listenbee, the advisory committee created by Attorney General Holder released a report pertaining to criminal jurisdiction over non-tribal individuals. Obviously, we deal with the Violence Against Women Act.

What else do we need to do to make sure we are getting justice for crimes committed against children? Do we need to do more to reform the system?

Mr. LISTENBEE. As regards to jurisdictional issues, those are certainly very important issues. Having just received the report on November 18th, we are reviewing those recommendations and trying to make some decisions about how best to address that particular issue going forward.

Earlier, you asked about suicide prevention. I want to bring to your attention that we have tribal youth programs that have been around since 2010. At that time we were funded at a level of $25 million a year to focus on developing youth leadership. We have been doing that since then.

Funding has gone down to the $5 million level but we nevertheless bring young people together, we talk to them about leadership roles, we have regional leadership groups and national leadership groups.

At those meetings, we do training on suicide prevention for all the youth who are involved. This seems to have had a positive effect on youth as they have indicated to us. We think this is one of the important ways we can address this issue.

You asked earlier about activities on actual reservations. We support mentoring programs on reservations. We think these are also very helpful. We have Boys and Girls Clubs on some of the reservations.

I would also like to bring to your attention that the Office of Violence Against Women has more than $30 million in programs in Alaska. Many of them are in the rural communities and villages. They are focusing on developing shelters for women in those areas. Those are some of the only shelters available for women to address those specific issues.

Senator CANTWELL. Thank you.

I have to go vote. I will look forward to following up with you on the details of those resources. I will turn it over to Senator Franken.

Senator FRANKEN. [Presiding] Thank you. I guess I am the chairman. I recognize Senator Franken.

Thank you, Senator Franken.

[Laughter].

Senator FRANKEN. I am sorry I couldn't be here, I had to vote, obviously but I thank you for your testimony.

I have a question that is open to anyone. I would think Dr. van den Pol and Mr. Listenbee may have something to say about this.

This is about the cultural or historic circled trauma as a concept. What is the history of that in terms of when was that identified or named or understood to be part of what children or anyone in Indian Country faces?

I understand it is now included in the list of traumas in this and this is mainly about childhood trauma but when was that named? What is the history of that?

Mr. LISTENBEE. On that matter, I would have to defer to Ms. Enomoto or to Dr. van den Pol.

Dr. VAN DEN POL. Senator Franken, I can't tell you the first published study that discussed historical trauma. I can attempt to conceptualize historical trauma with a broader understanding of trauma.

For example, part of the definition clinically is that trauma is a personal sense of being overwhelmed by a horrific circumstance. Two individuals experiencing the same automobile accident with the same injuries, one may be traumatized and the other may not.

You have to ask and that is one of the things that makes early assessment and early screening difficult if a young child doesn't have the verbal skills to answer questions about intrusive thoughts or insomnia, for example, whereas an adult might.

With historical trauma, when we talk to Native people, many of them express trauma symptoms regarding loss of land, loss of ancestors, broken treaties, lies that were told and that distress isn't slight, it is considerable. It is clinically significant.

While academics currently debate the putative validity of the concept of historical trauma, Native people experience it and as a consequence, I am convinced it is real. I don't think the first publications using that term were more than 20 or 25 years ago. Conversation about trauma began in Vietnam but trauma in children began really at the end of the 1990s.

Senator FRANKEN. Ms. Enomoto, did you want to speak? Anyone can speak to this. I am the chairman. Oh, you are the chairman. I yield myself infinite amount of time.

Ms. ENOMOTO. Administrator Listenbee noted that SAMHSA has recently issued a concept of trauma and guidelines for trauma in practice. In that, we outline three Es for trauma: how to define the individual experience of trauma. First, there is an event or a series of events which a person perceives as potentially life threatening or which result in physical or emotional harm.

There is the experience of that event. As Dr. van den Pol noted, it could be how the individual perceives or lives through that event and then the long term adverse effects of that event.

For two children who are bullied at school, you might imagine that one child who is raised in a nurturing home with safe and stable relationships might have more resilience and coping skills in order to address that bullying whereas another child who has been physically or sexually abused, who has witnessed domestic violence or who has been bounced around from multiple foster homes might not be able to deal with that bullying in the same way.

As the science tells us, our bodies are biologically primed to react to the world as a more dangerous and threatening place if we have experienced multiple adverse events and we have been stimulated in that fight or flight mode over time.

You can imagine that historical trauma, while there are these broad political, social, cultural, legal wrongs that have occurred, also translate into very concrete actions. The first reports on the boarding schools, for example, from the 1960s outlined terrible crimes against young children and families.

In my recent visit to Fort Belknap, I heard a very sad story about someone's grandmother who was sent away to boarding school at a very young age. But the gentleman I was talking with said, but she couldn't read. I said, ''she went to boarding school, oh, they didn't learn anything there''. They were subjected to forced labor, to significant abuse, to the degradation of their culture and their language.

When these young children are removed from their homes for three, four, five or ten years and then return home, how can they reintegrate into their families? How can they become parents when their experience of childhood and their upbringing was by strangers, by abusive adults, by people who were supposed to be trusted who actually violated that trust?

Those experiences, while historical, play out in families, in homes, in communities. Whether it is the historical trauma of the Holocaust, the historical trauma of slavery or the historical trauma of the Indian boarding schools, you can see where those things can play out in the homes of families with the next generation who grow up to witness people who have difficulties with attachment, substances, mental illness and so on.

Senator FRANKEN. Mr. Chairman, may I have a little bit more time.

The CHAIRMAN. [Presiding.] Yes.

Senator FRANKEN. I have no doubt that historical trauma is a big piece of this. The way you define it was how your actions affects seven generations down. There is historical trauma in a lot of different senses. One is what a parent does can traumatize.

I noticed in your attachments that the definition of trauma is normal reaction to an abnormal event. These are adverse childhood experiences we are talking about.

What I wanted to get to is that if the idea of, the history of cultural trauma, historical trauma is new, I would like to say that I also think about the absence of cultural identity, the absence of a language, and the absence of a cultural identity.

I am Jewish. I am not a terribly devout Jew but I know I am Jewish and it is very much a part of my identity. I probably went into comedy in no small part because I am Jewish. It means a lot to me and who I am.

What I have heard from you and read from you, Mr. Listenbee, is about culturally sensitive treatments. What I want to know is how old that is, what is the history of that and how do we measure, how do we begin to measure the effects of that, define it and define how we use that because I think that is terribly important.

Mr. LISTENBEE. I am not an expert on this issue so I will make one brief comment about it.

The science of adolescent development has grown tremendously in the last two decades. Neurosciences have grown. Our ability to actually watch the brain as it responds to different types of stimuli, using a variety of new tools that have come on line in the last two decades.

That science has become powerful enough so that the United States Supreme Court in several major decisions has relied upon the science of adolescent development and the neurosciences that accompany it.

I can tell you that these are new sciences for us. We are trying and tasked by the various experts with which we deal to do as much research as we can to better understand how adolescent development is derailed by trauma. We know that it is but we don't know always how to get children back on task.

We know that trauma informed care helps but it is still a new field. We do know we are heading in the right direction. We know that trauma for American Indian and Alaska Native children derails their normal development. We know a lot of the things science is telling us can help us get back on line.

That is enough to be dangerous, but it is what I know and what I have learned from really great experts when I worked with the Attorney General's National Task Force on Children Exposed to Violence.

I would add one other thing. Those experts told us this. They said that all American children should be assessed to determine whether they have experienced trauma at every important juncture, when they go to school, when they go to see their pediatricians, and if they have experienced trauma and it has derailed their normal development, what we need to do is get them trauma informed care.

That is what I know. I know that from the experts but if you take me farther than that, Senator, I would have to turn to my esteemed colleagues on the panel to explain the mechanics of it.

The CHAIRMAN. We would love to have you do that except the next vote has been called, so I think we have to wrap this up. I know I look like I run the 100 in less than 10 seconds but I don't.

I just want to thank the panel members for being here. Those of you who have traveled long distances, a special thank you. The hearing record will remain open for two weeks. There will be some written questions. You have been a great wealth of information, all of you. I just want to thank you all for being here today.

With that, the hearing is adjourned.

[Whereupon, at 3:53 p.m., the Committee was adjourned.]

APPENDIX

PREPARED STATEMENT OF RALPH FORQUERA, EXECUTIVE DIRECTOR, SEATTLE INDIAN HEALTH BOARD

Chairman Tester and members of the Senate Committee on Indian Affairs, my name is Ralph Forquera. I am the Executive Director for the Seattle Indian Health Board in Seattle Washington. The Health Board is an urban Indian health organization partially funded by the Indian Health Service. We provide direct and enabling health services for urban American Indians and Alaska Natives in Western Washington.

One of the services offered here at the Health Board is mental health counseling. In the last year, with expansion of the Medicaid program under the Affordable Care Act, the Health Board has likewise expanded its mental health services to better serve Indian youth. Over the years, we have been acutely aware of mental health problems among our urban Indian youth. Many face enormous social challenges being an Indian living in a city. This often shows up at school where we continue to see a high drop out rate among Indian youth and declining academic performance starting at the middle school. We are also aware that some Indian youth turn to gangs as a way of finding protection from bullying, and as a source of identity. For Indian girls, this can often result in sexual abuse or in some instances, coercion into prostitution and drugs.

As noted during a recent visit by Chairman Tester to our agency, urban Indians continue to be a mostly invisible population. Local resources including law enforcement and the public schools are ill prepared to address the social and cultural challenges that Indian youth face. The Health Board itself has limited resources to reach Indian youth. The fact that they are geographically dispersed throughout the metropolitan area means that finding Indian youth and offering emotional support is difficult. For the few that we work with, we know that there are many that remain without the proper attention needed.

Urban Indians are often overlooked when legislation regarding Indians is considered. For example, urban Indians are not included in the Violence Against Women Act directives for Indian Country. Funding through the Indian Health Service is limited to the single line item in the annual budget, so funds allocated for specific Indian health needs, like mental health, may not be available for urban Indians. We do receive a small grant for mental health generally from the Indian Health Service, but the resource is limited. With more than 7 out of 10 Indians now living in cities, according to the 2010 United States Census, a large number of Indian youth are living in cities without adequate social, cultural, or clinical support.

Cities provide unique mental health challenges for Indian youth. In most cases, the small number of Indians in any given region of a major city makes their presence almost invisible. In schools. there are seldom more than a feNA students and often, they come from different tribes with different cultural roots. Because some come from families where educational success was not likewise achieved, nearly a quarter of the Indians in the Seattle School District are enrolled in special education. While well meaning to get extra help for an Indian student, by placing an Indian youth in special education, the child may find this label added to other labels that may negatively reflect on their self-image. These unintended consequences of educational strategies are only appreciated by the Indian community. Without guidance from the community to recognize these cultural differences, a school district may not think to consider these matters when addressing the educational needs of native students.

While a growing percentage of native youth live in loving homes with supportive families, others are not so fortunate. In cities like Seattle, the cost of living is quite high and the educational demands for reasonable employment are extensive. In this vane, we often find Indian children without proper parental supervision or living in conditions that are not conducive to sound mental and emotional health. Drugs, alcohol, violence, and the insecurity that comes from poverty afflict a significant number of Indian youth. The ability to concentrate in school may be compromised by hunger or the emotional scars of an unsafe life.

Statistics are scarce regarding urban Indians. As a mostly invisible population, statistics related to Indians in cities is often lumped in the "other" category denying local leaders of important information to help plan and advocate for assistance. The small number of Indian youth in any single school district makes educational assistance difficult. Funding for Indian education, like other safety net services has declined over the last few decades while need has grown. Until and unless groups like the Senate Committee on Indian Affairs demand that local municipalities and other government institutions collect and analyze data on urban Indians and provide adequate support, the population will remain invisible and help will never reach those most in need.

Mental health is a serious health epidemic among Indian people both on and off reservation. The effects of untreated mental health problems is witnessed in incarceration, domestic and sexual violence, drug abuse and alcoholism, suicide, poor school performance, high—school drop out rates starting in middle school, and the many manifestations that accompany mental and emotional disharmony. We share the concerns of the members of the Senate Committee on Indian Affairs that there is a grave need to expand mental health services for Indian youth. Please remember as you deliberate that many of these youth live in American cities. Addressing youth mental health must reach beyond the reservation boundaries to American cities if the crisis in mental health among Indian youth is to be effectively addressed.

Thank you.

———

PREPARED STATEMENT OF RRICHA MATHUR, POLICY RESEARCH ASSOCIATE/PROGRAM MANAGER, FIRST FOCUS

Chairman Tester and Vice Chairman Barrasso, we thank you for the opportunity to submit this statement for the record in response to the recent Committee hearing on *"Preventing and Addressing Childhood Trauma in Indian Country."*

The First Focus Campaign for Children is a bipartisan advocacy organization dedicated to making children and families a priority in federal policy and budget decisions. Our organization is committed to promoting policies that serve the best interest and safety of children in the child welfare system. As you know, child abuse and neglect often contribute to long-lasting trauma in children and can impede child wellbeing and healthy development. We are concerned, as you are, by data and reports pointing to disproportionality in incidence of child abuse and neglect on Indian reservations and hope we can identify and promote effective and appropriate programs and services to address maltreatment for this vulnerable population.

A number of societal factors contribute to child abuse and neglect on Indian reservations. In 2009, 32.4 percent of American Indian children under the age of 18 lived in poverty. Unemployment rates for AI/AN adults are 14.6 percent—almost double that of White unemployment rates nationally.[1,2] 2 Financial instability can often strain families and reduce a parent's ability to manage stress and respond appropriately to a child. It can often mean that a parent feels unable to meet the needs of his or her child(ren). There is also a high propensity for sexual violence, substance abuse and trafficking on tribal lands due in part to a historic lack of law enforcement on Indian reservations.[3] AI/AN women are 2.5 times more likely to experience sexually violent crimes that other women.[4] These factors and others place AI/AN children at an increased risk for abuse and neglect and must be addressed.

A recent Department of Justice report, *Ending Violence so Children can Thrive,* authored by the Attorney General's Advisory Committee on American Indian/Alaska Native Children Exposed to Violence, underscores the urgent need for additional resources and supports for this population of children. The Committee found that AI/AN children experience violence at higher rates than any other race in the United States and face significant issues due to trauma resulting from exposure to violence.

"The immediate and long term effects of this exposure to violence includes increased rates of altered neurological development, poor physical and mental health, poor school performance, substance abuse, and overrepresentation in the juvenile justice system. This chronic exposure to violence often leads to toxic stress reactions and severe trauma; which is compounded by historical trauma." [5]

We fully support the Committee's efforts and would like to highlight several key recommendations included in its report:

1.3 Congress should restore the inherent authority of American Indian and Alaska Native (AI/AN) tribes to assert full criminal jurisdiction over all persons who commit crimes against AI/AN children in Indian country.

Comment: Tribes must be given the authority to adjudicate crimes in their territories to deter violence from occurring and to impose penalties on those who commit crimes against children. The lack of enforcement by federal authorities to prosecute criminals in these areas and the powerlessness of the tribal courts to hold perpetrators responsible has historically attracted criminals to Indian country. Much of the trauma experienced by AI/AN children is the result of violence and empowering tribes to carry out justice on their lands will help reduce the incidence of violence, and therefore trauma and services needed.

1.4 Congress and the executive branch shall direct sufficient funds to AI/AN tribes to bring funding for tribal criminal and civil justice systems and tribal child protection systems into parity with the rest of the United States and shall remove the barriers that currently impede the ability of AI/AN Nations to effectively address violence in their communities.

Comment: Tribal programs are underfunded and many problems with the judicial and child protection programs cannot be solved until more money is invested in these programs. The United States, as a trustee of tribal lands and resources, has an obligation to ensure the wellbeing of AI/AN tribes. Specifically, increases in funding should be made for the Department of Interior: Welfare Assistance and Indian Child Welfare Act On-Reservation Programs and the Department of Health and Human Service's Promoting Safe and Stable Families and Child and Child Welfare Services programs.

2.1 The legislative and executive branches of the federal government should ensure Indian Child Welfare Act (ICWA) compliance and encourage tribal-state ICWA collaborations.

Comment: A *recent policy brief* authored by the National Indian Child Welfare Association identifies ICWA's key requirements as:

1) Encouraging more intensive examination of the efforts to prevent removals of AI/AN children and rehabilitate their parents,
2) Improving the identification of tribal and relative families who can serve as placement resources for AI/AN children,
3) Increasing access to culturally appropriate services,
4) Clarifying roles between states and tribes in child welfare matters,
5) Increasing sharing of funding and other resources between states and tribes, and
6) Stimulating the development of state policy to improve the effectiveness of services and supports for AI/AN children and families.

Unfortunately, implementation of these requirements has been varied and the purpose of these provisions is not being met. Lack of oversight by federal authorities as well as limited resources appropriated have made it difficult for ICWA to reach its potential.[6]

2.6 The Secretary of Health and Human Services (HHS) should increase and support access to culturally appropriate behavioral health and substance abuse prevention and treatment services in all AI/AN communities, especially the use of traditional healers and helpers identified by tribal communities.

Comment: Adults with substance abuse and behavioral health issues can endanger the lives of surrounding children in their communities as well as those in their care. Investments must be made in preventative services to strengthen families so that children are not exposed to violence, abuse, and neglect in the first place and to empower members of tribes through resources and culturally appropriate trainings so they can provide services to their peers. In addition, funding and access to mental health services by AI/AN children is essential. Investments should continue to be made in the Children's Mental Health Initiative system of care grants and the Children and Family Programs circle of care grants.

Moving forward, we believe the swift and effective implementation of all of the Committee's recommendations is vital to improving the lives of AI/AN children.

An all too common response to the violence and trauma AI/AN children experience is to place them in the foster care system. Yet there are practice concerns that need to be addressed. AI/AN children are three times more likely to be reported to child protective services and twice as likely to remain in foster care for more than two years than their non-AI/AN peers. For example, in North Dakota, AI/AN make up 9 percent of the population, but 30 percent of the state's child abuse victims.7 This overrepresentation of AI/AN children in foster care can be, in part, attributed to a bias in the system, leading child protective services to view certain cultural practices as child neglect or abuse, or view AI/AN families as less likely to benefit from family preservation or alternate response, services and supports that would keep them out of the foster care system, or even perhaps, that these families are inherently more likely to be abusive and criminal and removal of a child is almost always the right choice.

ICWA addresses some of these concerns by recognizing the important role of tribes in removal and placement decisions and by providing protections to keep AI/AN families safely together and children connected to their communities and cultures. However, widespread non-compliance with ICWA and a lack of adequate services and supports for American Indian families continues to place high numbers of American Indian children at risk of removal and entry into the foster care system.

We are encouraged by Attorney General Holder's December 3rd announcement that the Department of Justice is launching a new initiative to promote compliance with ICWA. States are also working to implement pieces of ICWA into their state codes by incorporating new AI/AN specific definitions, ensuring notification to AI/AN parents and tribes of custody proceedings, and increasing collaborations between states and tribes. States are also issuing guidance to providers and relevant agencies to encourage compliance with ICWA.8 We hope that Congress will do its part as well and make the necessary resources available to aid the Administration in this important effort.[9]

We thank you again for the opportunity to submit this statement for the record and look forward to working with you to ensure that the recommendations put forth by the Attorney General's Advisory Committee are fully implemented.

■ ■ ■ ■ ■ ■ ■ ■ ■ ■ ■ ■ ■ ■

[1] Aspen Institute, Fast Facts on Native American Youth and Indian Country (Sept. 2013), Available at *http://www.aspeninstitute.org/sites/default/files/content/images/Fast%20Facts.pdf.*

[2] Simmons, David, *Improving the Well-Being of American Indian and Alaska Native Children and Families through State-Level Efforts to Improve Indian Child Welfare Act Compliance* (Sept. 2014). Available at: *http://www.nicwa.org/government/documents/Improving%20the%20Well-being%20of%20American%20Indian%20and%20Alaska%20Native%20Children%20and%20Families\2014.pdf*

[3] Substance Abuse among American Indian or Alaska Native Adults, June 24, 2010. Available at *http://www.samhsa.gov/data/2k10/182/AmericanIndian.htm*

[4] Patricia T jaden and Nancy Thoennes, *Full Report of the Prevalence, Incidence, and Consequences of Violence Against Women*, pg. 23. Available at *https://www.ncjrs.gov/pdffiles1/nij/183781.pdf.*

[5] U.S. Department of *Ending Violence So Children Can Thrive*, Attorney General's Advisory Committee on American Indian and Alaska Native Children Exposed to Violence (Nov. 2014), Available at *http://www.justice.gov/sites/default/files/defendingchildhood/pages/attachments/2014/11/18/finalaianreport.pdf*

[6] Simmons, David, *Improving the Well-Being of American Indian and Alaska Native Children and Families through State-Level Efforts to Improve Indian Child Welfare Act Compliance*, pg. 4 (Sept. 2014). Available at: *http://www.nicwa.org/government/documents/Improving%20the%20Wellbeing%20of%20American%20Indian%20and%20Alaska%.20Native%20Children%20and%20Families\2014.pdf*

[7] Tomothy Williams, Officials See Child Welfare Dangers on a North Dakota Indian Reservation (July 7, 2014), Available at *http://www.nytimes.com/2012/07/08/us/child-welfare-dangers-seen-on-spiritlakereservation.html?pagewanted=all&lr=0*

[8] Simmons, David, *Improving the Well-Being of American Indian and Alaska Native Children and Families through State-Level Efforts to Improve Indian Child Welfare Act Compliance*, pg. 9 and 10 (Sept. 2014). Available at: *http://www.nicwa.org/government/documents/Improving%20the%20Wellbeing%20of%20American%20Indian%20and%20Alaska%20Native%20Children%20and%20Families\2014.pdf*

[9] Attorney General Eric Holder Delivers Remarks During the White House Tribal Nations Conference, Dec. 3 2014. Available at: *http://www.justice.gov/opa/speech/attorney-general-eric-holder-delivers-remarks-during-white-house-tribal-nations*

PREPARED STATEMENT OF GWENDOLYN PURYEAR KEITA, PH.D., EXECUTIVE
DIRECTOR/PUBLIC INTEREST DIRECTORATE, AMERICAN PSYCHOLOGICAL ASSOCIATION

Dear Chairman Tester and Vice Chairman Barrasso:

On behalf of the nearly 130,000 members and affiliates of the American Psychological Association (APA), I want to commend your leadership in holding the November 19, 2014 Oversight Hearing on "Protecting our Children's Mental Health: Preventing and Addressing Childhood Trauma in Indian Country."

APA has a longstanding commitment to improving conditions in Indian country and increasing access to mental health resources for our most vulnerable populations. This is especially true as it pertains to the need to better understand and address childhood trauma issues in American Indian/Alaska Native (AI/AN) communities. The hearing underscores the necessity for Congress to redouble its efforts to invest in prevention, early intervention, and treatment programs and services for Native American youth.

We applaud your inclusion of psychologist Rick van den Pol, Ph.D., of the National Native Children's Trauma Center at the University of Montana on the witness panel. Dr. van den Pol's center is funded by the Substance Abuse and Mental Health Services Administration under the National Child Traumatic Stress Network which plays an instrumental role in developing effective evidence-based treatments and resources to better help traumatized children, their families and communities cope and heal.

Moreover, as mentioned in the hearing, there exists a substantial need to increase the number of and retain culturally competent psychologists in tribal communities. Among the most valuable of initiatives to address this provider shortage is the *Indians into Psychology* (InPsych) program, first authorized in 1992. This vital program creates educational and mentorship opportunities for AI/AN students who are interested pursuing careers in psychology. We hope that Congress will support this vital program and expand its funding as called for through the reauthorization of the Indian Health Care Improvement Act in 2010 in the Affordable Care Act.

Our association stands ready to be a resource to the Senate Indian Affairs Committee and your offices. We look forward to working with you in the 114th Congress to ensure child trauma issues and provider training in Indian Country remains a legislative and oversight priority. .

PREPARED STATEMENT OF THE NATIONAL INDIAN CHILD WELFARE ASSOCIATION
(NICWA)

The National Indian Child Welfare Association (NICWA) is a national American Indian and Alaska Native (AI/AN) nonprofit organization located in Portland, Oregon. NICWA has provided technical assistance and training to tribes, states, and federal agencies on issues pertaining to child maltreatment, Indian child welfare, children's mental health, and juvenile justice for over 30 years. NICWA is a leader in the development of public policy that supports tribal self-determination in child welfare, children's mental health, and juvenile justice systems, as well as compliance with the Indian Child Welfare Act (ICWA). NICWA also engages in research to support and inform services and policy for AI/AN children and families. NICWA is the nation's most comprehensive source of information on AI/AN child maltreatment, child welfare, and children's mental health issues.

We would first like to thank the committee members for their interest in the well-being of AI/AN children and families. There is no effort more important than the protection of AI/AN children, the prevention of childhood exposure to violence, and the treatment of trauma. This hearing was called in response to the Department of Justice (DOJ) Report issued by the Attorney General's Advisory Committee on AI/AN Children Exposed to Violence titled *Ending Violence So That Children Can Thrive*. This testimony will review critical areas where AI/AN children are exposed to violence and highlight the most important related recommendations in the report.

It is our sincere hope that this hearing is the beginning, and not the end, of this crucial conversation. Tribes work tirelessly to keep their children safe but there is still much that the federal government can do to support these efforts.

Child Protection

Civil Cases
The prevention of, and response to, child abuse and neglect in Indian Country involves many different governments, service providers, and governmental systems. Without coordination at each step, families' needs can go unmet and children can be left in danger (Cross, 2005). At the heart of the problem are jurisdiction and funding.

In P.L. 280 states, tribes face unique jurisdiction and service responsibility challenges when child protection systems respond to reports of child abuse and neglect. The issue of whether states have concurrent jurisdiction with tribes on tribal lands in P.L. 280 areas has not been fully resolved. Further, many states believe they have concurrent jurisdiction on tribal lands—a troubling position that some courts have affirmed. Where concurrent jurisdiction has been asserted, jurisdictional authority and service responsibility can be uncertain. This often result in delays in civil (child protection/child welfare) responses to reports of child abuse involving AI/AN children on tribal lands.

Some tribes in P.L. 280 states have been able to develop intergovernmental agreements to address these jurisdictional and service responsibility challenges. Due to some states' reluctance or unwillingness to negotiate agreements, many tribes have not been able to develop agreements and confusion continues. Although ICWA provides for the re-assumption of civil child welfare and child protection jurisdiction (25 USC § 1918), the current process is very burdensome and can take two or more years to complete.

Although all tribes recognize the importance of prevention, and many provide programs that incorporate child abuse prevention activities, they do so with little or no federal support. Furthermore, the prevention work they do is in communities with families that are at a higher-than-average risk for child abuse and neglect. Tribes do have access to some funds that are flexible and can be used to prevent and intervene in child maltreatment cases. Due to the limited funding available for tribal child welfare generally, available flexible funding sources are often used to support non-prevention, non-child protection crisis management services.

Key Taskforce Recommendations
- **Recommendation 1.4.B.** Congress shall appropriate, not simply authorize, sufficient substantially increased funding to provide reliable tribal base funding for all tribal programs that

impact AI/AN children exposed to violence. This includes tribal criminal and civil justice systems and tribal child protection systems. At a minimum, and as a helpful starting point, Congress shall enact the relevant funding level requested in the National Congress of American Indians (NCAI) *Indian Country Budget Request for FY2015*.

- o Comment: Funding must provide flexible opportunities that allow tribes to design their child welfare services to meet the needs of their children and families. Priority programs include:
    - Department of the Interior (DOI): Indian Child Protection and Family Violence Prevention child abuse prevention and treatment grant programs ($43 million in authority)
    - Department of Health and Human Service (DHHS): Community-Based Child Abuse Prevention ($60 million); Child Abuse Discretionary Activities ($35 million)
- o The grant provisions of the Indian Child Protection and Family Violence Prevention Act (P.L. 101-630) must be fully funded. Since this law's passage in 1991, no federal agency has requested funding for its three authorized grant programs. Consequently, Congress has never appropriated funds for these critical programs. These grant programs are the only funds dedicated for tribal governments to support (1) child abuse treatment; (2) child abuse prevention and investigation of child abuse reports; (3) family violence prevention and treatment services; and (4) the establishment of Indian child resource and family service centers to assist tribes with the investigation and prevention of, as well as treatment for, victims of child abuse and domestic violence.
- o The Child Abuse Prevention and Treatment Act contains funding for states to provide community-based child abuse prevention and other child abuse discretionary activities. Tribal governments, however, are only eligible for a minuscule amount of these funds. Tribal child abuse prevention funds come through a 1% set-aside that tribes share with migrant populations that amounts to two tribal grants every three years of approximately $300,000.

- **Recommendation 1.7.** The legislative and executive branches of the federal government should encourage tribal-state collaborations to meet the needs of AI/AN children exposed to violence.
    - o Comment: The Bureau of Indian Affairs (BIA), in consultation with tribes, must reform the process for tribal re-assumption of civil child welfare/child protection jurisdiction in P.L. 280 states under ICWA 25 U.S.C. § 1918.
    - o Comment: Congress must establish a mandate for P.L. 280 states to negotiate the development of intergovernmental agreements that address jurisdictional and service responsibility challenges in child welfare "in good faith" with tribes.

Criminal Cases

An important part of protecting children from violence and preventing trauma includes the ability to prosecute all individuals who perpetrate crimes of sexual and physical abuse against children. These individuals pose a serious risk to the safety to the community and its children. The complicated scheme that governs jurisdiction in criminal cases committed in Indian Country can be summarized as follows:

Not "Major" Crimes Non-P.L. 280

Persons Involved	Jurisdiction non-P.L. 280 state
Indian accused, Indian victim	Tribal government
Indian accused, non-Indian victim	Tribal government and federal government
Non-Indian accused, Indian victim	Federal government
Non-Indian accused, non-Indian victim	State government

"Major" Crimes Non-P.L. 280

Persons Involved	Jurisdiction non-P.L. 280 state
Indian accused, Indian victim	Tribal government and federal government
Indian accused, non-Indian victim	Tribal government and federal government
Non-Indian accused, Indian victim	Federal government
Non-Indian accused, non-Indian victim	State government

All crimes P.L. 280

Persons Involved	Jurisdiction P.L. 280 State
Indian accused, Indian victim	State government and tribal government
Indian accused, non-Indian victim	State government and tribal government
Non-Indian accused, Indian victim	State government[1]
Non-Indian accused, non-Indian victim	State government

In general, the complexity of this scheme is often cause for prosecutions to fall through the cracks. The most significant gap in this jurisdictional scheme is that any crime committed by a non-Indian against an Indian cannot be prosecuted under tribal jurisdiction. Unfortunately, when it comes to non-P.L. 280 states, the federal government declines to prosecute the majority of these crimes. According to figures compiled by the Transactional Records Access Clearinghouse at Syracuse University, prosecutors declined 52% of cases involving serious crimes in Indian Country. Specifically, the government rejected 61% of cases involving charges of sexual abuse of children. In contrast, the Justice Department declined 20% of drug trafficking cases nationwide (Williams, 2012). Although the Violence Against Women Act (VAWA) Reauthorization Act of 2013 corrected for this problem in situations of domestic violence, it did not include provisions for child abuse, and does not recognize the jurisdiction of Alaska Native villages. This means that currently, cases of sexual abuse by a non-Indian offender against an AI/AN children often go unprosecuted.

Key Taskforce Recommendations
- **Recommendation 1.3.** Congress should restore the inherent authority of AI/AN tribes to assert full criminal jurisdiction over all persons who commit crimes against AI/AN children in Indian Country.
- **Recommendation 5.1.D.** Congress should repeal Section 910 of Title IX of the VAWA Reauthorization Act of 2013, and thereby permit Alaska Native communities and their courts to address domestic violence and sexual assault committed by tribal members and non-Natives just as in the lower 48 states.
- **Recommendation 5.1.E.** Congress should affirm the inherent criminal jurisdiction of Alaska Native tribal governments over their members within the external boundaries of their villages.

Child Welfare Intervention

Tribes have an important relationship with their children and families: they are experts in the needs of AI/AN children, best suited to effectively serve those needs, and most able to improve child welfare outcomes for these children (National Indian Child Welfare Association & Pew Charitable Trust, 2007). Self-determination is necessary to good outcomes for AI/AN children and families.

Essential to successful tribal child welfare is law that provides tribes the freedom to design and implement programs that meet their community's needs, culturally competent support and technical assistance from federal agencies, and a budget that avoids unnecessary restraint to tribal decision making. Best practice in tribal child welfare is shown in the following diagram where the sloping line signifies the amount of time and resources necessary for a given intervention.

---

[1] In 2013, the Violence Against Women Act extended criminal jurisdiction to tribes to ensure that non-Indian perpetrators of interpersonal violence could be prosecuted in tribal courts.

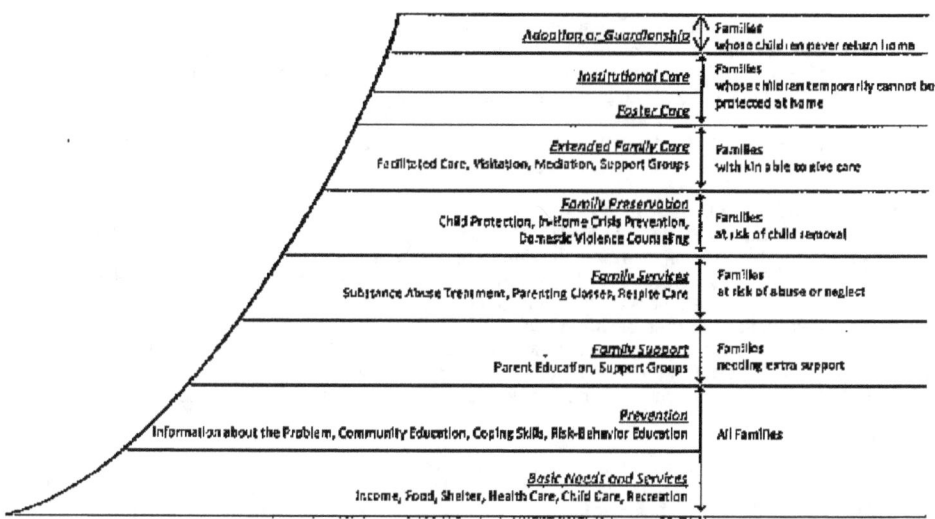

Currently tribal child welfare is grossly underfunded and the funds that are available are heavily biased toward foster care and permanency outside the home. Unfortunately, funding for tribal child welfare resembles an inverse configuration of the diagram above where more of the resources are located at the end of the child welfare process (removal from home and permanent placements outside the home) instead of where services can be useful in preventing maltreatment and removal from the home.

Key Taskforce Recommendations

- **Recommendation 1.4.B.** Congress shall appropriate, not simply authorize, sufficient substantially increased funding to provide reliable tribal base-funding for all tribal programs that impact AI/AN children exposed to violence. This includes tribal criminal and civil justice systems and tribal child protection systems. At a minimum, and as a helpful starting point, Congress shall enact the relevant funding level requested in the NCAI *Indian Country Budget Request for FY2015.*
  - Comment: Funding must provide flexible opportunities that allow tribes to design their child welfare services to meet the needs of their children and families. Priority programs include
    - DOI: Welfare Assistance (\$80 million), Indian Child Welfare Act On-Reservation Program (Tribal Priority Allocation—\$15.6 million; Self-Governance—\$16.5 million)
    - DHHS: Promoting Safe and Stable Families (\$76 million discretionary; \$345 million mandatory), Child Welfare Services (\$280 million)
  - Comment: Congress should reform federal child welfare financing. The new funding measures should create a balanced and sustainable base of funding for tribes and states. Reform should focus on supporting the prevention of child maltreatment and in-home services that strengthen families to reduce the need for out-of-home placements. Additional resources should be provided specifically to tribal communities for treatment services that address childhood trauma, parental substance abuse, and historical and present day trauma experienced by many parents.

- **Recommendation 2.2.** The BIA in the DOI, the Administration for Children and Families (ACF), and tribes, within one year of the publication of this report should develop and submit a written plan to the White House Domestic Policy Council, to work collaboratively and efficiently to provide trauma-informed, culturally appropriate tribal child welfare services.
- **Recommendation 2.3.** The ACF of the DHHS, BIA in the DOI, and tribes should collectively identify child welfare best practices and produce an annual report on child welfare best practices in AI/AN communities that is easily accessible in tribal communities.

Indian Child Welfare Act Compliance

Family "is the single most important survival mechanism of [AI/AN] culture; it follows that Indian child welfare practice should focus on the home and family as its most important point of intervention" (Cross, 1995a, p. 3). Yet AI/AN children continue to be removed from their homes at alarming rates, even though "formal foster care services are still foreign to Indian culture" (Cross, 1995b, p. 3). This culturally inappropriate intervention is extremely traumatic for AI/AN children and families. Removal and foster care should be "the last line of defense after all attempts have been made to strengthen the family so that a child can remain in his or her own home" (Cross, 1995b, p. 5).[2] This, however, is not how state systems work with AI/AN children and families, in spite of the requirements present in ICWA that mandate this practice.

ICWA requires state child welfare agencies to provide active efforts to support Native families so that children can safely remain in their homes. When removal is necessary, ICWA mandates that states place Native children in family and tribal foster care. ICWA also provides tribes, like states, the opportunity to participate in child welfare decisions involving their citizen children and families. Where ICWA is followed, AI/AN child welfare goals are met. These successes include safety, permanency, child well-being, and family well-being (Limb, Chance, & Brown, 2004). State child welfare systems and private adoption systems, however, are straying from the requirements of the law. There is recent research documenting non-compliance with most of the key provisions of ICWA.

Non-compliance is likely due to the fact that there is minimal oversight of ICWA implementation. ICWA was enacted without providing sanctions for non-compliance, incentives for effective compliance, a data collection requirement, or a mandate for an oversight committee or authority to monitor compliance.

Key Taskforce Recommendations

- **Recommendation 1.4.B.** Congress shall appropriate, not simply authorize, sufficient substantially increased funding to provide reliable tribal base funding for all tribal programs that impact AI/AN child welfare systems. At a minimum, and as a helpful starting point, Congress shall enact the relevant funding level requested in the NCAI *Indian Country Budget Request for FY2015*.
  - *Comment:* Priority programs:
    - DOI: Indian Child Welfare Act On-Reservation Program (Tribal Priority Allocation—$15.6 million; Self-Governance—$16.5 million); Indian Child Welfare Act Off-Reservation Program ($5 million)
- **Recommendation 2.1.** The legislative and executive branches of the federal government should ensure ICWA compliance and encourage tribal-state ICWA collaborations.
  - *Comment:* The executive branch must follow up in states where there is knowledge of ICWA non-compliance. When ACF becomes aware of ICWA non-compliance via Child and Family Service Reviews or other sources, it should take action to assess the source

---

[2] Added to this equation is the legacy of removal that AI/AN children have faced. For nearly a century, AI/AN children were removed from their homes and placed in residential schools where formal education was used as an assimilation tactic (Jones, Tilden, & Gaines-Stoner, 2008). For decades in the 1900s, AI/AN children were systemically removed from their homes and placed in white homes without good cause or due process in an effort to assimilate (Jones, Tilden, & Gaines-Stoner, 2008). Each removal of an AI/AN child from her home, family, and community is an act of violence. Unfortunately, AI/AN children are often subjected to this violence; AI/AN children are overrepresented in foster care at rates that exceed all other populations in the United States (Summers, Woods, & Donovan, 2013).

and scope of non-compliance and provide assistance to states to improve ICWA compliance.
- o *Comment:* The executive branch must improve monitoring of tribal-state relations in child welfare, and increase efforts to educate states about the benefits of tribal-state collaboration and best practice models that are working. Incentivizing state participation in these efforts to improve service coordination and collaboration is also necessary.

- **Recommendation 2.1.A.** Within two years of the publication of this report, the ACF in the DHHS, BIA in the DOI, and tribes should develop a modernized, unified data-collection system designed to collect Adoption and Foster Care Analysis Reporting Systems and ICWA and dependency data on AI/AN children who are placed in foster care by their agency and share that data quarterly with tribes to allow tribes and the BIA to make informed decisions regarding AI/AN children.
  - o Comment: Initially, states must be required to collect ICWA data. This may be done as part of existing data collection measures, but can also be done in separate data collection activities (Adoption and Foster Care Analysis and Reporting System and National Child Abuse and Neglect Data System). States are already required to report a variety of measures on the children in their care. Requirements pertaining to ICWA, including a determination of ICWA eligibility, tribal notification, active efforts provided, placement according to placement preference, and other concerns related to AI/AN child welfare, should be added to these requirements. Including ICWA information in state reporting requirements would provide the information necessary to improve federal oversight and evaluate national ICWA compliance. These data will ultimately help target resource allocation and areas needing further policy development.

- **Recommendation 2.1.B.** The Secretaries of the DOI and DHHS should compel BIA and ACF to work together collaboratively to collect data regarding compliance with ICWA in state court systems. The ACF and BIA should work collaboratively to ensure state court compliance with ICWA.
  - o *Comment:* ACF should contract with ICWA experts to perform a thorough review of the ICWA compliance measures states are currently using. The results of this review should be compiled into comprehensive best practice documents and a toolkit for states to use to increase nationwide ICWA compliance. There is currently no national source of comprehensive information on the innovative ICWA compliance measures states are taking and the creative tribal-state collaborations occurring. Collecting and disseminating this information will help states think creatively about what they could do to ensure ICWA compliance.

- **Recommendation 2.1.C.** The BIA should issue regulations (not simply guidelines) and create an oversight board to review ICWA implementation and designate consequences of non-compliance and/or incentives for compliance with ICWA to ensure the effective implementation of ICWA.
  - o *Comment:* We commend the BIA's efforts to review and revise the ICWA *Guidelines for State Courts* originally created in 1979. The goal of the review should be to include requirements in the form of regulations to the extent legally defensible. The guidelines are designed to help state courts effectively implement ICWA. Nonetheless, there are numerous case law examples of courts disregarding the best practices, definitions, and interpretation delineated in the guidelines. Regulations, which carry different legal authority, cannot be so readily ignored. Translating the guidelines, to the extent possible, into regulations will improve ICWA compliance.

- **Recommendation 2.1.D.** The DOJ should create a position of ICWA specialist to provide advice to the Attorney General and DOJ staff on matters relative to AI/AN child welfare cases, to provide support in cases before federal, tribal, and state courts, and to coordinate ICWA training for federal, tribal, and state judges, prosecutors, and other court personnel.
  - o *Comment:* Currently, the DOJ engages in ICWA litigation via amicus curiae briefs which are written and filed by the Environment and Natural Resources Division of the Department of Justice. This department, however, lacks necessary expertise in family law and in ICWA specifically. For these reasons, the DOJ should create a special counsel position for Indian child welfare. Furthermore, because ICWA violations are themselves civil rights violations, as well as intricately entwined with larger issues of bias in the child welfare system. This position, therefore, should be placed in the Civil Rights Division

where they can monitor and engage in on-going litigation as well as affirmatively investigation, litigate, and remedy ICWA non-compliance.
- o *Comment:* The DOJ should conduct an ICWA compliance investigation. The levels of disproportionality, particularly in states with high AI/AN populations, and the studies that show bias treatment of AI/AN families in state child welfare and private adoption systems allude to systemic civil rights violations of AI/AN children and families, DOJ's Civil Rights division must look into these troubling practices.

Children's Mental Health Services

Today, AI/AN children and communities grapple with complex behavioral health issues at higher rates than any other community. Mental health issues are not only the product of childhood violence and trauma, they are also often the impetus for adults perpetrating violence on or in the presence of AI/AN children. When children's mental health is not addressed directly it only perpetuates the cycles of violence.

To understand the behavioral health needs of AI/AN children and youth, the legacy of trauma that has been visited upon this population must be recognized. Past treatment has left AI/AN people with unresolved historical trauma (Yellow Horse Brave Heart and DeBruyn, 1998) and in socially and geographically isolated communities that rank at the bottom of a number of socioeconomic indicators (NCAI, 2012)—all risk factors for mental and behavioral health issues. Resources to address mental health needs in tribal communities are currently insufficient. Inadequate funding, uncoordinated health systems, and a shortage of mental health professionals are key barriers to the development of successful interventions (Novins & Bess, 2011).

Some tribes have begun to create integrated family- and youth-driven, culturally and linguistically competent, strength-based child welfare programs that are successfully meeting the mental health needs of youth. These models take years to create and substantial infrastructure to support.

Key Taskforce Recommendations

- **Recommendation 1.4.B.** Congress shall appropriate, not simply authorize, sufficient substantially increased funding to provide reliable tribal base funding for all tribal programs that impact AI/AN children exposed to violence. This includes tribal criminal and civil justice systems and tribal child protection systems. At a minimum, and as a helpful starting point, Congress shall enact the relevant funding level requested in the NCAI *Indian Country Budget Request for FY2015.*
  - o *Comment:* Funding must provide flexible opportunities that allow tribes to design their children's mental health services to meet the needs of their community. Priority programs include:
    - DHHS: Programs of Regional and National Significance: Children and Family Programs ($6.5 million), and Children's Mental Health Services Program: Children's Mental Health Initiative ($117 million); Tribal Behavioral Health Grants ($5 Million)
- **Recommendations 2.6** The Secretary of Health and Human Services should increase and support access to culturally appropriate behavioral health services in all AI/AN communities, especially the use of traditional healers and helpers identified by tribal communities.
  - o *Comment:* Tribal system of care (system of care and circle of care) initiatives are essential children's mental health programs that should be supported to the fullest extent and specifically authorized.
    - Children's Mental Health Initiative system of care grants support a community's efforts to plan and implement strategic approaches to mental health services and supports that are family-driven; youth-guided; strengths-based; culturally and linguistically competent; and meet the intellectual, emotional, cultural, and social needs of children and youth. Since 1993, 173 total projects have been funded, dozens of which have been in tribal communities. Currently, 17 tribal communities are currently funded.
    - The Children and Family Programs circle of care grants provide funding for the same work as the system of care program. This grant program, however, is the

only SAMHSA grant program that is focused specifically on AI/AN children's mental health needs. It is also the only SAHMSA program that allows tribes and tribal organizations to apply without competing for funding with other governmental entities such as states, counties, or cities. There are currently seven communities receiving circle of care funding. This grant program must be specifically authorized to ensure tribal access to these important funds.

Juvenile Justice

AI/AN youth are over-represented in state and federal juvenile justice systems and secure confinement (Arya & Rolnick, n.d.). In fact, disproportionality is present for AI/AN youth at each stage of the delinquency process nationwide, with the exception of arrests (Arya & Rolnick, n.d.). Anecdotal evidence suggests that incarcerated AI/AN youth in general are much more likely to be subjected to the harshest treatment in the most restrictive environments and are less likely to have received the help they need from other systems.

Treatment of Indian youth is complicated by the multi-jurisdictional framework applicable to AI/AN juveniles involved with the justice system. Depending on where activity occurs and the nature of the activity, an Indian youth can be subject to federal, state, or tribal law. ICWA recognizes that tribes have unique rights that must be preserved regarding the placement of their children and the continuity of their families. Currently, in the case of status offenses, ICWA applies to AI/AN youth who may be removed from their families through the state court system. The act provides safeguards for AI/AN youth who may be placed outside of their home by mandating tribal notification in those proceedings and the possibility for transfer to tribal court. The well-known failure of state courts to apply ICWA's protections to AI/AN juvenile status offenders who have been removed or are at risk of being removed from their homes undermines the rights of tribes as sovereign nations. Where the juvenile act constitutes a crime, however, the safeguards of ICWA do not come into effect.

Key Taskforce Recommendations

- **Recommendation 4.1.** Congress should authorize additional and adequate funding for tribal juvenile justice programs, a grossly underfunded area, in the form of block grants and self-governance compacts that would support the restructuring and maintenance of tribal juvenile justice systems.
- **Recommendation 4.1.B.** Federal funding for state juvenile justice programs should require that states engage in and support meaningful and consensual consultation with tribes on the design, content, and operation of juvenile justice programs to ensure that the programming is imbued with cultural integrity to meet the needs of tribal youth.
- **Recommendation 4.4.** Federal, tribal, and state justice systems should only use detention of AI/AN youth when the youth is a danger to themselves or community. It should be close to the child's community and provide trauma-informed, culturally appropriate, and individually tailored services, including reentry services. Alternatives to detention such as "safe houses" should be significantly develop in AI/AN urban and rural communities.
- **Recommendation 4.6.** Congress should amend ICWA to provide that when a state court initiates any delinquency proceeding involving an Indian child for acts that took place on the reservation, all of the notice, intervention, and transfer provisions of ICWA apply. For all other children involved in state delinquency proceedings, ICWA should be amended to require notice to the tribe and the right to intervene. At first step, the Department of Justice should establish a pilot project that would provide funding for three states to provide ICWA-type notification to tribes within their state whenever the state court initiates a delinquency proceeding against a child from that tribe which includes a plan to evaluate the results with an eye toward scaling it up for all AI/AN communities.
  - *Comment:* ICWA should be amended to ensure that states recognize tribes' jurisdictional authority over delinquency proceedings involving an Indian child for acts that took place on the reservation. It should also be amended to provide that where a state court has obtained jurisdiction over such acts, pursuant to federal law, and the state court initiates any delinquency proceeding involving an Indian child for acts that took place on the reservation, all of the notice, intervention, and transfer provisions of ICWA will apply. For all other Indian children involved in state delinquency proceedings, ICWA should be amended to require notice to the tribe, a right to intervene, and transfer provisions. The

act shall also provide for a set of preferences. The first preference shall be release of the child to his or her parents, relatives, or another placement that does not involve confinement. Where that is not possible, the preferences should provide for a placement that is rehabilitative with a preference for tribal facilities, followed by a program approved by the child's tribe near the child's family and tribe.

- o *Comment:* DOJ, BIA, and ACF should develop an initiative to improve state education and compliance with current provisions in ICWA that provide for the protections of notice, intervention, transfer, and to the extent applicable, placement provisions for Indian children who are in state juvenile justice systems for status offenses. The Office of Juvenile Justice and Delinquency Prevention should increase education efforts and create a data collection/oversight mechanism to ensure compliance with this already existing, but underutilized juvenile justice protection.

References

Arya, N. & Rolnick, A. C. (n.d.) *A tangled web of justice: American Indian and Alaska Native youth in federal, state, and tribal justice systems.* Washington, DC: Campaign for Youth Justice.

Cross, T. L. (1995a). *Heritage & helping: A model curriculum for Indian child welfare practice, Module II: Protective services for Indian children.* Portland, OR: National Indian Child Welfare Association.

Cross, T. L. (1995b). *Heritage & helping: A model curriculum for Indian child welfare practice, Module IV: Family-centered services for Indian children.* Portland, OR: National Indian Child Welfare Association.

Cross, T. L. (2005). Child abuse prevention in Indian Country. In D. S. Bigfoot, T. Crofoot, T. L. Cross, K. Fox, S. Hicks, L. Jones, & J. Trope (Eds.), *Impacts of child maltreatment in Indian Country: Preserving the seventh generation through policies, programs, and funding streams.* Portland, OR: National Indian Child Welfare Association.

Jones, B. J., Tilden, M., & Gaines-Stoner, K. (2008). *The Indian Child Welfare Act handbook: A legal guide to the custody and adoption of Native American children.* Chicago, IL: ABA Publishing.

Limb, G. E., Chance, T., & Brown, E. F. (2004). State compliance with Indian Child Welfare Act to improve outcomes for American Indian families and children. *Protecting Children, 18(3),* 13–23.

National Congress of American Indians. (n.d.). *Indian country demographics content.* Retrieved from http://www.ncai.org/about-tribes/demographics

National Indian Child Welfare Association & Pew Charitable Trusts. (2007). *Time for reform: A matter of justice for American Indian and Alaska Native children.* Philadelphia, PA: Pew Charitable Trusts.

Novins, D. K., & Bess G. (2011). 10. Systems of mental health care for AI/AN children and adolescents. In P. Spicer, P. Farrell, M. C. Sarche, & H. E. Fitzgerald (Eds.), *AI/AN children and mental health: Development, context, prevention, and treatment.* Santa Barbara, CA: SABC-CLIO, LLC.

U.S. Department of Health and Human Services, Administration for Children and Families, Administration on Children, Youth and Families, Children's Bureau. (2010e). *Child maltreatment 2008.* Rockville, MD: U.S. Department of Health and Human Services.

U.S. Department of Health and Human Services, Administration for Children and Families, Administration on Children, Youth and Families, Children's Bureau. (2013a). *Child maltreatment 2012.* Rockville, MD: U.S. Department of Health and Human Services. Retrieved from http://www.acf.hhs.gov/programs/cb/resource/child-maltreatment-2012

Yellow Horse Brave Heart, M. & DeBruyn, L. M. (1998). The American Indian Holocaust: Healing historical unresolved grief. *American Indian Mental Health Research, 8(2),* 56–78.

––––––––

RESPONSE TO WRITTEN QUESTIONS SUBMITTED BY HON. JON TESTER TO RICK VAN DEN POL

Question. One of the stated goals of the National Native Children's Trauma Center is to significantly increase the cultural relevancy of the interventions it disseminates across Indian Country. In its trainings and consultations, how exactly does the Center work to ensure that cultural practices are incorporated into treatment for behavioral health?

Answer. In the thirteen years that we have been treating youth with trauma in Indian Country, we have seen a positive shift in the willingness of federal agencies to allow Native cultural practices to be included in evidence-based trauma treatment.

In about 2003, the 40-year old field of Implementation Science was not well understood. Implementation Science is concerned with "high fidelity" implementation of treatment protocols. Procedural deviations were considered methodological and clinical flaws. However, during the past five years Implementation Science has expanded to include "treatment optimality," and the inclusion of cultural practices has proven an excellent fit within a framework of treatment optimality research.

In fact, when we first began including Elders and Healers in school-based trauma treatment we expected criticism from the field and from our sponsors for failing to have a high fidelity trauma treatment protocol. But currently when we speak of treatment optimality, we find strong support among our peers, editors and grant officials. At the November 2014 SCIA Oversight Hearing, it was truly dramatic to hear officials from SAMHSA and OJJDP explain that they uniformly support treatment innovations that include cultural practices.

"While not conducive to short-term change, we have developed three developmental approaches that seem to support long term relationships with Tribes and tribal members. First, we only work in communities where we have been invited. Second, we consider that all data resulting from tribal partnerships are the property of the Tribe; the Tribe may or may not give us permission to disseminate those data. Third, in addition to protecting individual identity, we do not disclose the identity of a Tribe unless the Tribe asks us to do so."

"We also have found it valuable to engage local community members in participatory dialog regarding their perceptions of the value of treating childhood trauma, what the outcomes of successful trauma treatment should look like, and whether there already are traditional support strategies that could be blended with the evidence-based trauma treatment. While some local adaptations have been procedural (e.g., inviting students to draw a picture to supplement their oral trauma narrative), we also have invited local cultural experts to contribute traditional language and traditional healing strategies during group trauma treatment."

"In some communities, our early efforts to include traditional Native language and culture stimulated apprehensions among our tribal partners. One set of concerns involved the proprietary nature of Native language and culture. Closely linked were perceptions that researchers might exploit or otherwise profit from information shared by healers and Elders. (And because we do this work as part of our university employment, we cannot completely nullify this perception.)"

"To date, no Tribe has refused our request to share results of trauma treatment. However, the extent to which we discuss traditional language and culture follows one of three protocols. Which protocol is followed is determined by Tribal Council decision with recommendations from Elders. In the first case, traditional language and healing ceremonies are made available to children and youth who choose them, but whether and how that occurs is not disclosed in our dissemination. In the second case, we report that a community volunteer with expertise in language and culture participated in the trauma treatment program, but the intervention(s) he or she used are not recorded, named or described. In the third case, the traditional ceremony may be named and may be described. In every case, we inform the Tribal Council of our findings before disseminating elsewhere."

(Reprinted from Whitegoat, W. and van den Pol, R. 2014. Cultural adaptations of trauma treatments in Indian Country, CW 360 Trauma Informed Child Welfare Practice, Winter 2013, 25, 38.)

RESPONSE TO WRITTEN QUESTIONS SUBMITTED BY HON. JON TESTER TO VERNÉ BOERNER

1) Have the various telehealth programs currently in use in many Alaska Native communities been utilized to address childhood trauma? If so, how?

Response:

There is a need for more and a great need for additional telemental and telebehavioral health programs for most Alaska Native communities. The Alaska Native Health Board consulted with the Alaska Federal Health Care Access Network (AFHCAN) program administered by the Alaska Native Tribal Health Consortium (ANTHC). The AFHCAN program provides telehealth services to Alaska Natives and American Indians beneficiaries across the State. At this time, there is no telehealth program specific to childhood trauma within the AFHCAN system. However, some tribal partners in the Alaska Tribal Health System have developed their own telemental and telebehavioral health programs, and created business relationships with providers within and outside of Alaska. Some of these programs may have a childhood trauma program or protocol. A query of each of program individually would be necessary to determine the extent of such programs, if any.

Given the depth of the problem of childhood trauma among Alaska Natives, including the large percentage of Alaska Native youth who have been removed from their homes and are in foster care and other homes, such a program would be a very helpful addition to the AFHCAN system, we welcome the opportunity to have a discussion with the Committee on ways to expand the capacity of tribal health and other programs to address this problem.

While there is no specific telehealth childhood trauma program, Alaska tribes are training providers on methods to address trauma. Therefore certain capacities and approaches are already in place that could be incorporated into a comprehensive and collaborative approach that includes telemental and telebehavioral health. Such activities include:

- The AFHCAN program works with the State of Alaska in multiple venues to investigate the utilization of telehealth to support the Sexual Abuse Response Teams (SART) and the SART nurses in providing care to victims of sexual abuse.
- The AFHCAN technology is shared with other IHS and Tribal health programs, and is being used to document abuse and trauma in multiple regions throughout the US, most recently in Montana.
- AFHCAN works closely with regional partners, such as SouthCentral Foundation (SCF), to develop telehealth approaches. For example, more than a decade ago SCF and AFHCAN developed the capacity to use telehealth to support the diagnosis of Fetal Alcohol Syndrome by a team of specialists.

The AFHCAN program also shared the following description of a the IHS-funded Alaska Native Epidemiology Center's (EpiCenter's) trauma related approach currently in place, undertaken in conjunction with the state of Alaska programs, to specifically provide services to teenagers who are the victim of trauma:

The Alaska Native Epidemiology Center (EpiCenter) provides health-related data and resources to promote education and preventative care for a variety of issues, including domestic and sexual violence. EpiCenter staff is adapting and helping implement an evidence-based and trauma-informed approach tailored to address domestic and sexual violence in Alaska. This work comes at a critical time -- the Alaska Victimization Survey has found that 59 percent of women in Alaska have experienced physical violence, sexual violence or both in their lifetimes, and studies have also shown that Alaska's rate for childhood trauma is the highest in the country EpiCenter staff offers training and technical assistance on this approach for Alaska health care providers and staff at Alaska Tribal Health System organizations, in partnership with the State of Alaska Family Violence Prevention Project. The approach uses a discreet, wallet-sized patient safety card developed specifically with and for Alaska Native teenaged girls and women. According to EpiCenter staff, the cards allow providers to address health and relationship issues in a manner that is more sensitive to the needs of survivors of violence. Is is a noninvasive approach to providing information about how relationships affect our health, one that does not require singling out individuals who are not ready to seek help or discuss the topic with a provider.

"What makes this approach more comfortable and effective than simply asking patients questions like 'Are you safe at home?' is that it focuses on building trust

with the patient," explained Laura Avellaneda-Cruz, an ANTHC Epidemiologist. "Providers can then offer information, resources and encourage the message that the patient is not alone, the abuse is not her fault, and there is help. Every patient, whether she chooses to disclose to her provider or not, still gets to walk away with something useful, either to keep for herself or to share with a friend."

EpiCenter staff, in partnership with the State of Alaska's Department of Adolescent Health and Family Violence Prevention Project, is currently creating a gender-neutral teen safety card that addresses issues of importance to teens around Alaska, particularly Alaska Native teens. Teens from around Alaska will provide guidance and feedback as the card is created. Childhood hardships such as abuse or exposure to household violence can have lifelong and even intergenerational consequences. Research shows that with well-timed and well-implemented interventions, these lifelong issues can be alleviated and even prevented for many Alaska Native children.

To learn more about ANTHC's EpiCenter work with trauma-informed care and the safety card approach, contact ANTHC's Laura Avellaneda-Cruz at (907) 729-2489 or at ldavellanedacruz@anthc.org. Learn more about the EpiCenter's work on domestic and sexual violence and request safety cards at the EpiCenter's Healthy Families' Project page, www.anthctoday.org/epicenter/healthyfamilies. Learn more about the State of Alaska's Family Violence Prevention Project at http://dhss.alaska.gov/dph/Chronic/Pages/InjuryPrevention/akfvpp/default.aspx.

RESPONSE TO WRITTEN QUESTIONS SUBMITTED BY HON. MARK BEGICH TO VERNÉ BOERNER

1) Ms. Verné Boerner – Thank you for being here as a witness, and for your work at the Alaska Native Health Board.

   o We have heard from numerous witnesses for the past 12-18 months about repealing Section 910 of VAWA.
   o From your view point at ANHB, why is that provision is so detrimental?

A top priority for Alaska Native tribes and communities is the right to self govern so that we can best provide services for our people. Tribes in Alaska and across the nation have long demonstrated that self-governance is effective and efficient. Tribes have quickly built capacity on various new, challenging, and complex issues. Tribes run programs efficiently and are responsive to the communities. Repealing Section 910 of the Violence Against Women Reauthorization Act of 2013 (VAWA) provides tribes with additional tools with which to address violence against women, which, as you know, is of epidemic proportion. Studies have shown that the health of women has direct correlation to the health of the family and overall communities and my personal experience, as I testified, is a stark example of this.

Tribal communities believe in taking holistic approaches and put great emphasis on restoration on balance and harmony. Such approaches when taken together not only affect the judicial system, but also the health of a community.

The Alaska Native Health Board applauds both you and Senator Lisa Murkowski for your efforts for bringing to fruition the repeal of Section 910 of the Violence Against Women Reauthorization Act of 2013.

Response to the following questions was not available at the time this hearing went to print

WRITTEN QUESTIONS SUBMITTED BY HON. JON TESTER TO KANA ENOMOTO

Question 1. In your testimony you mention your agency recently awarded 20 Tribal Behavioral Health grants to tribes to develop and implement plans that address suicide and substance abuse. Do you have any idea how many tribes currently have a youth suicide prevention plan?

Question 2. You've been working on trauma with SAMHSA for over a decade now. What have been some of the biggest steps forward in the Agency's efforts to address trauma? In your opinion, what still needs to be done within the Agency?

Question 3. Could you briefly discuss how SAMHSA has made sure that its programs for Native communities are culturally informed?

WRITTEN QUESTIONS SUBMITTED BY HON. TOM UDALL TO KANA ENOMOTO

Question 1. I see value in the Tribal Behavioral Health grant program, where each tribe can develop and implement behavioral health interventions best suited for their own members. However, with 566 federally recognized tribes, 20 grants do not go a long way. How can SAMHSA reach more tribes with this program?

Question 2. As research is revealing more effective tools and strategies for screening and identifying those who have experienced historical trauma, what is the capacity of the screeners to know how to respond and refer?

Question 3. Are there sufficient places for treatment that these children and their family members (if appropriate) can/will be referred to?

Question 4. What can be done to address the need for effective treatment as effective screening will increase the demand for such services?

Question 5. The services, programs and funding of IHS, SAMHSA and DoJ are all vital to help prevent, identify, refer and treat Native Americans and Alaska Natives for mental health and childhood trauma issues. How are these (and any other federal agencies) working together to coordinate efforts so that tribes benefit from synergy of these efforts, and that federal definitions, screening tools, practice guidelines, funding streams and other aspects of these activities are coordinated, streamlined, flexible and consistent federally?

Question 6. Given the extent of the problem and the actual appropriations currently available, what proportional increase would be required to address closer to 90 percent of the need?

Question 7. While biomarker and interview screening can help identify people at risk for behavioral health problems based on historical trauma, children re-experience the trauma of feeling worthless when we send them to schools that are crumbling and unsafe, and health clinics and hospitals that are dilapidated and out of date.

Question 8. What are you doing to end this form of trauma by creating environments that reflect the worth and value of Indian children through every encounter with your services?

WRITTEN QUESTIONS SUBMITTED BY HON. MARK BEGICH TO KANA ENOMOTO

Question 1. It has been noted by HHS's Health Resources and Service Administration that there are apx 4,000 mental health shortage areas across the country, many of which are in Native communities.

Question 2. Can you talk a bit about how technology is being incorporated to close these gaps?

Question 3. How effective has tele-health been in closing these national gaps?

WRITTEN QUESTIONS SUBMITTED BY HON. JON TESTER TO
HON. ROBERT L. LISTENBEE, JR.

Question 1. Childhood trauma is an issue that many departments are attempting to address. How have agencies and departments ensured adequate coordination between initiatives?

Question 2. DOJ, SAMHSA, and IHS mentioned using videos, hotlines, and outreach publicity campaigns to address trauma prevention and treatment. How are we measuring ''success'' and effectiveness in these programs and campaigns?

Question 3. How does the shortage of Native mental health care providers impact the delivery of trauma treatment services?

Question 4. Communities often seek to integrate traditional healing practices into programs aimed at addressing trauma. What obstacles exist that limit or prevent the inclusion of such practices?

Question 5. You're funding evaluations in two tribal communities, including one in my home state of Montana with on the Rocky Boy's Reservation. Many of our tribal communities in Montana have been hit hard by the sudden deaths of young people—through accidents, through substance use, through suicide, and through violence. While I applaud the effort to build the body of research, how do we ensure that we're actually making a difference in tribal communities? How are we measuring success in the face of such extreme and immediate need?

Question 6. How is your office making sure that tribes have the technical resources to compete for grants—particularly for smaller tribes?

Question 7. How are the DOJ and OJJDP's Native trauma efforts reaching Native kids who live off reservation in urban communities? What resources are available for that population?

Question 8. Unfortunately, the DOJ works with many Native kids who are both victims and victimizers. What is the DOJ doing to make sure that Native children held in federal prisons and institutions are receiving treatment for previously experienced trauma?

Question 9. In August of this year, I held a listening session on Human Trafficking in Indian Country at the Fort Peck Reservation in Montana. Although there have been Indian communities struggling against these heinous crimes for years, in my State of Montana, the uptick in the trafficking industry is has been truly disturbing. The historical trauma you mention in your testimony makes our Native communities even more vulnerable to trafficking. As your office funds the National Center for Missing & Exploited Children, I'm wondering if you can provide us some more information on how it is increasing coordination with tribes to provide them tools to combat against traffickers.

Question 10. Much of the prosecution of trafficking crimes is under the jurisdiction of States. What type of outreach to State attorneys general and prosecutors are being undertaken by the Department to combat trafficking in Indian Country?

WRITTEN QUESTIONS SUBMITTED BY HON. TOM UDALL TO
HON. ROBERT L. LISTENBEE, JR.

Question 1. The services, programs and funding of IHS, SAMHSA and DoJ are all vital to help prevent, identify, refer and treat Native Americans and Alaska Natives for mental health and childhood trauma issues. How are these (and any other federal agencies) working together to coordinate efforts so that tribes benefit from synergy of these efforts, and that federal definitions, screening tools, practice guidelines, funding streams and other aspects of these activities are coordinated, streamlined, flexible and consistent federally?

Question 2. Given the extent of the problem and the actual appropriations currently available, what proportional increase would be required to address closer to 90 percent of the need?

Question 3. While biomarker and interview screening can help identify people at risk for behavioral health problems based on historical trauma, children re-experience the trauma of feeling worthless when we send them to schools that are crumbling and unsafe, and health clinics and hospitals that are dilapidated and out of date.

Question 3a. What are you doing to end this form of trauma by creating environments that reflect the worth and value of Indian children through every encounter with your services?

WRITTEN QUESTIONS SUBMITTED BY HON. MARK BEGICH TO
HON. ROBERT L. LISTENBEE, JR.

Question. Mr. Listenbee, I very much appreciate your background on the various DOJ programs. I see there are a handful of pilot or demonstration projects currently in place that sound fantastic, but that are only set up in 2 or 3 tribal communities. How does the DOJ envision expanding these demo projects over the next 3–5 years, once there is evidence-based data showing their effectiveness?

———

WRITTEN QUESTIONS SUBMITTED BY HON. JON TESTER TO
HON. YVETTE ROUBIDEAUX

Question 1. What does the IHS do to recruit and retain mental health providers that specialize in children's mental health?

Question 2. What is the current vacancy rate for mental health providers at the IHS? Please provide a detailed breakdown of the vacancies by region and position.

Question 3. Is the current funding for children's mental health treatment and youth suicide prevention sufficient?

Question 4. You mentioned the importance of ensuring that efforts to address trauma in Indian Country are coordinated across agencies. How does IHS coordinate with other agencies, NGOs, etc., to ensure the biggest impact is made?

Question 5. Your testimony mentioned a new comprehensive national Child Maltreatment policy for IHS. When can we expect to see this new policy rolled out? What initiatives and changes will such a policy include?

Question 6. How does the IHS attempt to integrate traditional healing practices into its mental health and trauma treatment plans?

WRITTEN QUESTIONS SUBMITTED BY HON. TOM UDALL TO
HON. YVETTE ROUBIDEAUX

Question 1. It has been noted by HHS's Health Resources and Service Administration that there are approximately 4,000 mental health shortage areas across the country, many of which are in Native communities. Can you talk a bit about how technology is being incorporated to close these gaps?

Question 1a. How effective has tele-health been in closing these national gaps?

Question 2. Dr. Roubideaux, in your testimony you note that IHS has had over 15,000 tele-health substance abuse and mental health encounters in the last 5 years. How does IHS measure the success rate of these encounters?

Question 3. Dr. Roubideaux, you note several times in your testimony that over 50 percent of Mental Health, Alcohol and Substance Abuse funds are transferred under 638 contracts to tribes/tribal organizations that run their own programs. Does IHS have a system in place to evaluate the success/outcomes of tribally managed programs?

Question 3a. Is there a system in place that allows IHS to incorporate and design federally managed programs, based on tribal models that are proven to be effective?

WRITTEN QUESTIONS SUBMITTED BY HON. MARK BEGICH TO
HON. YVETTE ROUBIDEAUX

Question 1. The services, programs and funding of IHS, SAMHSA and DoJ are all vital to help prevent, identify, refer and treat Native Americans and Alaska Natives for mental health and childhood trauma issues. How are these (and any other federal agencies) working together to coordinate efforts so that tribes benefit from synergy of these efforts, and that federal definitions, screening tools, practice guidelines, funding streams and other aspects of these activities are coordinated, streamlined, flexible and consistent federally?

Question 2. Given the extent of the problem and the actual appropriations currently available, what proportional increase would be required to address closer to 90 percent of the need?

Question 3. While biomarker and interview screening can help identify people at risk for behavioral health problems based on historical trauma, children re-experience the trauma of feeling worthless when we send them to schools that are crumbling and unsafe, and health clinics and hospitals that are dilapidated and out of date. What are you doing to end this form of trauma by creating environments that reflect the worth and value of Indian children through every encounter with your services?

www.ingramcontent.com/pod-product-compliance
Lightning Source LLC
Chambersburg PA
CBHW081142290526
45795CB00006B/2335